Dad,

Thank you for your many years of love, support and encouragement. This wouldn't have been possible without you.

Love,

Brandon

International Political Economy Series

Series editor
Timothy M. Shaw
Visiting Professor
University of Massachusetts
Boston, USA

and

Emeritus Professor at the University of London, UK

The global political economy is in flux as a series of cumulative crises impacts its organization and governance. The IPE series has tracked its development in both analysis and structure over the last three decades. It has always had a concentration on the global South. Now the South increasingly challenges the North as the centre of development, also reflected in a growing number of submissions and publications on indebted Eurozone economies in Southern Europe. An indispensable resource for scholars and researchers, the series examines a variety of capitalisms and connections by focusing on emerging economies, companies and sectors, debates and policies. It informs diverse policy communities as the established trans-Atlantic North declines and 'the rest', especially the BRICS, rise.

More information about this series at
http://www.springer.com/series/13996

Brandon Tozzo

American Hegemony after the Great Recession

A Transformation in World Order

Brandon Tozzo
Trent University
Peterborough
PE, Canada

International Political Economy Series
ISBN 978-1-137-57538-8   ISBN 978-1-137-57539-5 (eBook)
https://doi.org/10.1057/978-1-137-57539-5

Library of Congress Control Number: 2017940215

© The Editor(s) (if applicable) and The Author(s) 2018
The author(s) has/have asserted their right(s) to be identified as the author(s) of this work in accordance with the Copyright, Designs and Patents Act 1988.
This work is subject to copyright. All rights are solely and exclusively licensed by the Publisher, whether the whole or part of the material is concerned, specifically the rights of translation, reprinting, reuse of illustrations, recitation, broadcasting, reproduction on microfilms or in any other physical way, and transmission or information storage and retrieval, electronic adaptation, computer software, or by similar or dissimilar methodology now known or hereafter developed.
The use of general descriptive names, registered names, trademarks, service marks, etc. in this publication does not imply, even in the absence of a specific statement, that such names are exempt from the relevant protective laws and regulations and therefore free for general use.
The publisher, the authors and the editors are safe to assume that the advice and information in this book are believed to be true and accurate at the date of publication. Neither the publisher nor the authors or the editors give a warranty, express or implied, with respect to the material contained herein or for any errors or omissions that may have been made. The publisher remains neutral with regard to jurisdictional claims in published maps and institutional affiliations.

Credit: Rob Friedman/iStockphoto.com

Printed on acid-free paper

This Palgrave Macmillan imprint is published by Springer Nature
The registered company is Macmillan Publishers Ltd.
The registered company address is: The Campus, 4 Crinan Street, London, N1 9XW, United Kingdom

Acknowledgements

I would like to acknowledge numerous people for their support throughout this project. This project has been in the making for a long time, with much of it influenced by my dissertation work at Queen's University in Kingston, Ontario. In particular, I would like to thank my supervisor Phillip Wood who guided me throughout my research and offered hours of advice on a wide array of academic and non-academic issues. I am certainly a better student, writer, researcher and teacher thanks to his supervision. I would also like to acknowledge my colleagues at the Political Studies Department at Trent University for their support during the project. I am also grateful to my students, especially those in my American politics class, who always keep me thinking and regularly challenge my assumptions about the USA.

I would like to thank Timothy Shaw and the editors at Palgrave Macmillian for their time, patience and help in this project. Writing a book was quite an undertaking and it would have been impossible without their assistance.

I would also like to thank the United States Department of State for admitting me into the US Visitor's Leadership Program during the 2016 US states federal election. It was an experience of a lifetime to conduct interviews in Washington, D.C., Louisiana and Ohio during the height of the election season. I experienced the election of Donald Trump at the Republican headquarters in Cleveland, Ohio—an event I will never forget. It was a rare honour for an academic to be selected and the one I will treasure.

Thanks go to my long-time friends Dorian Mills and Robbyn Lindsay in London, Ontario for their moral support. I would like to recognize an incalculable debt to my family, Joseph and Jill Tozzo, Eleanor Hobden, Jamie and Kyra Ellington and Graham Tozzo. Without the love from my friends and family this would not have been possible. Finally, I would like to acknowledge my wife Jenna Willoughby for her years of love and patience as I went through this process.

Contents

1. An American Crisis; A Global Recession — 1
2. The Great Wars and the Post-war Consensus 1914–1979 — 13
3. The Neoliberal Orthodoxy 1979–2000 — 43
4. A Crisis in the European Union — 65
5. The Demographic and Economic Problems of China — 79
6. American Political Polarization and the Rise of Trump — 93
7. The Coming Global Crisis — 127

Bibliography — 135

Index — 153

CHAPTER 1

An American Crisis; A Global Recession

Since the end of the Second World War, the USA has been the dominant capitalist country in the international system. It has been central to the expansion of businesses into new markets and into new territories. While America has relied upon incentives, it also has at its disposal the most advanced military in the world to ensure the stability of the capitalist system. During the financial crisis of 2008, the USA was the source of crises, with the financial contagion spreading to the rest of the global economy. Since then, this superpower has been mired in poor economic growth with its political system seemingly unable to contend with these new problems. A relatively minor crisis in the American housing market has had far-reaching and dire ramifications in seeming unrelated parts of the world. The problems quickly spread to the Eurozone, which could soon be on the verge of collapse due to a series of sovereign debt crises. Even in East Asia, China has taken measures to ensure the continuity of its regime and the country's continued economic growth. The recession has highlighted that capitalism is a global system that interconnects disparate countries and peoples. And yet after all these difficulties with massive unemployment and an increase in poverty, reform of the financial system remains tentative and difficult. The costs of the crisis are borne by some of the poorest people, while investors and corporations receive tax cuts and government bailouts. Even the USA, the largest economy in the world, seemed unable to mitigate the effects of the recession.

The purpose of this book will be twofold: first, to explain the historical development of the financial system as a political project that conditions the response of political leaders to the Great Recession that began in 2007. Contrary to the Great Depression where a series of new domestic and institutional arrangements have been put in place, the outcome of the Great Recession was to reinforce the international status quo, with America remaining dominant (Helleiner 2014). While the power and influence of the financial industry is a contributing factor, there are far more complicated reasons for the inaction. In each region, the responses to the recession have been inhibited by the limitations of institutional arrangements dictating a series of policies, on the one hand, and pressure from financial markets and the financial industry to maintain the financialization of the system, on the other. In the immediate wake of the crisis, there was considerable political will to reshape the international financial system, but as the immediacy faded, orthodoxy remained, despite years of tepid economic growth in most OECD countries.

Secondly, and most critically, this book will intervene in a debate on the future of American hegemony. The response of the USA to the crisis has developed a contradiction: the main threat to American hegemony is not from the global capitalist system, nor from foreign competitors, but its political system. Since the Second World War, the USA has been the hegemon of the international capitalist system—promoting free trade, market liberalism and a central player in many international institutions. Polarization is common in American politics. The American public is divided on a wide array of social and economic issues: whether the state should promote school prayer, women's access to abortion, the role of government in health care and same-sex marriage. While each of these issues is significant in their own right, they have not had global ramifications. Since the onset of the Great Recession conflict has expanded into areas that were previously non-politicized or where there was cross-party consensus. With an increasingly ideologically divided Congress, the rise of the Tea Party, and the success of Donald Trump in 2016, Americans are now seriously debating whether the USA should remain committed to global free trade and open markets, and whether America should continue to maintain its role in institutions like NATO (the North Atlantic Treaty Organization). However, despite the politics, the USA currently has low unemployment, decreasing budget deficits and a booming stock market. Compared to other countries, the USA has come out the Great Recession in a stronger position than its major contenders. My analysis is not that America lacks the economic resources or policy tools to manage contradictions in capitalism or international crisis, but, the crisis has shown the

American political system is becoming increasingly unwilling due to politics. To put the overall thesis of this book succinctly, the greatest threat to American hegemony and the stability of global capitalism in the twenty-first century is America.

I will also provide an analysis of the major challengers on an international stage to American hegemony in order to show that they suffer from significant institutional, political and economic problems. In Europe, the institutional framework of the EU and the Euro has constrained both wealthier northern countries and the economically weak south. While the economic crisis in Southern European countries is abated through loans, along with austerity measures, politically, there is little popular will to increase the political unity of Europe. On the contrary, years of recession, a migration crisis from the Middle East and the rise of right-wing nationalist parties have made many Europeans far more sceptical of "Project Europe". The Recession has shown the fissures within the European Union, along geographic lines. In 2016, Britain voted for a "Brexit" from the European Union, and while the details have yet to be worked out, this is a worrying sign for future integration in Europe. It continues to be unlikely Europe will be able to seriously contend with the USA as a unified global superpower in the near future.

The other major contender that many expect to compete with the USA is one of its largest trading partners: China. While the country has experienced a dramatic economic transformation since it began opening in the late 1970s, China now faces a series of new problems as it tries to move from a middle-income country and "go global" (Shambaugh 2013). Certainly, the rapid development of China and other countries such as India and Brazil represents a shift in regional power towards these new, growing economies, but as of yet they lack the military or economic capacity to challenge the USA as a dominant actor on a global stage (Christensen and Xing 2016). China faces a series of economic, social, demographic and political problems that have undermined the optimism about its ascendency as a Superpower. The driving force behind China's policy prior to and during the recession has been due to its demographics. China must keep its economy growing in order for the regime to keep its legitimacy, thus it has kept buying American and even European debt to ensure global economic stability. Yet, there remain numerous questions about China's long-term stability and capacity for economic growth. Its domestic housing sector is overvalued in certain markets, while its stock market crashed in mid-2015 and has yet to recover. Furthermore, there are numerous social factors that could undermine its stability, including its ageing population placing pressure on the state, its demographic disparity between men and women due to China's One Child Policy, and dramatic unrest among its working population. Institutionally, the capacity of the Chinese Communist Party to maintain its control over the country is the case a protracted recession remains an open question, but at least several years on, it appears premature to suggest China has the capabilities to match, or overtake, the USA.

In the wake of crisis, there have been two major schools of thought on the future of the USA as the dominant country in the global capitalist system. The first group of so-called declinists, which include Zakaria (2009), Ferguson (2011), Friedman and Mandelbaum (2012), Bremmer (2012), Panitch and Gindin (2012), argue that American power is in relative or absolute decline, either due to foreign competitors or due to contradictions in capitalism. The "anti-declinist" group, which include Helleiner (2014), Vermeiren (2014), Prasad (2014) argue that America's decline is overstated. The USA remains a politically stable, economically affluent and militarily dominant country despite the recent protracted recession. While this book firmly belongs in the anti-declinist school of thought, it makes a significant observation that differs from the other scholars by examining the role of domestic politics on the long-term prospects of American hegemony.

The book will balance a comprehensive overview of the changes in the international economy since the recession with the domestic policies of each major region. It will provide an analysis of the globalization of the international economy: how global finance in particular no longer has political boundaries, but is transnational in scope. This book will evaluate how each region has responded to the crisis and offer some criticisms and policy suggestions based on what has been successful and where there have been failures.

I will rely on a series of distinct literature throughout this book that will help to examine the global economy as a whole and the domestic factors in each case study, borrowing much from the International Political Economy and Comparative Political Economy literature. In Chaps. 3 and 4, I will assess the problems in international capitalism that started just prior to the Great Depression, as well as the major reorganization of the international system that occurred after the Second World War. The interwar period was the most recent time there was a hegemonic vacuum in global politics. Britain had declined as a Great Power, and the USA was constrained by domestic institutions which prevented it from participating in European affairs and in the League of Nations. Then, I will evaluate the major economic and geopolitical conflicts of the Cold War, including the Korean and Vietnam wars. From there in Chap. 2, I will examine the origins of the decline of the Bretton Woods system of capital control and the rise of the neoliberalism in the 1980s. It will also outline the origins of the globalization of finance in the 1970s, which accelerated during the 1980s and 1990s. It will briefly discuss the periodic crisis caused by the financialization of the system, such as the peso crisis, the Southeast Asian crisis and the dot-com bubble. This will be followed by a discussion of the opening of the Chinese economy, and the collapse of the Soviet Union. By the 1990s, America was the lone superpower and neoliberal capitalism was popularized as the only path to economic prosperity.

In the year 2000, America was booming, China had joined the World Trade Organization, and countries in Europe adopted the Euro. However, shortly after the terrorist attacks of September 11th, 2001, problems started to arise. The USA began to accumulate massive deficits in the War on Terror, provided by Chinese financing. Countries opposed the US war in Iraq. Yet, the global economy for the most prospered due to low inflation, high growth, fuelled by debt, and cheap borrowing. By 2007, the USA entered a recession due to collapsing housing prices. By the summer of 2008, firms such as Bear Sterns and Lehman Brothers began to show signs of trouble. In September 2008, the US government decided to let Lehman Brothers fail, leading to a massive crisis in the global financial system. I will spend time discussing the causes of the crisis and the ramifications of it for the USA, the Eurozone and China. Initially governments throughout the G20 united in a coordinated response to the crisis, introducing stimulus packages and targeted bailouts. After the worst of the crisis abated, the response of each region began to differ in policies towards the recession.

The approach I will use recognizes that capitalism is a systemic and totalizing force, but that it must be discussed in its historical context to be appropriately understood. It is even more pertinent at this time when capitalism is in crisis and the developed world is mired in recession. Moreover, this section will reference the mainstream International Relations (IR), Comparative Political Economy (CPE) and the International Political Economy (IRE) literature. Scholars in mainstream IR often argue the

America promotes international stability, free markets and political liberalism; it is often viewed as benevolent, progressive and necessary in global politics.[1] IPE often integrates production and the capitalist system in their analysis, but shares a number of assumptions with IR, emphasizing the actions of the US government as the main agent that spreads capitalism.[2] The focus of these chapters will be a re-examination of the USA using Marxian analysis as a theoretical guide.

Chapter 4 will examine the Eurozone crisis and its ramifications for Europe's place as a potential competing superpower. The economic crisis has led to a series of bailouts from national governments. Since 2008, there has been a considerable increase in sovereign debt in the PIIGS (Portugal, Italy, Ireland, Greece and Spain). Prior to the recession, many of these economies could borrow cheaply, but now international confidence has turned against them. Although the crisis is economic, the limitations of the Euro limit the policy responses from national governments. Essentially, the PIIGS must undergo painful austerity measures as a condition of bailouts rather than lowering the price of their currency or inflating their way out of debt. The problems with Eurozone are institutional. Though there are methods to overcome the crisis, they are complicated by the institutional structure of the EU.

The 2008 financial crisis and the subsequent recession have highlighted the problems associated with trying to develop a common currency for a region as varied as the Eurozone. The 17 countries that use the Euro are bound by treaty commitments to abide by the policies set out by the European Central Bank (ECB), which sets interest rates for the Eurozone. Nonetheless, a true fiscal union does not exist between EU member-states. Guidelines do exist to limit overall debt-to-GDP ratios and curtail annual deficit spending, but the enforcement mechanism for these rules is weak, and is often disregarded by the more powerful countries in the EU.[3] At the national level, each country sets its own budget, allocates its resources according to its own priorities and accumulates its own sovereign debt. This has led to high degree of incoherence in European policy, as well as sparking a crisis between prudent northern European countries and the spendthrift south. In contrast their northern counterparts, Mediterranean governments chose to borrow cheaply using the favourable interest rates that they gained through the adoption of the Euro.

As a result of this borrowing and the crisis, a major sovereign debt crisis has occurred in Portugal, Italy, Ireland Greece and Spain (PIIGS), all of which, with the exception of Ireland, accumulated high levels of debt in the years prior to 2008. So far, it is the Greek economy that has teetered closest to a full default, reaching an unsustainable 140% debt-to-GDP ratio in 2011.[4] Financial markets, sensing that Greece is unable to carry such a large debt given the size of its economy fled Greek bonds, driving up borrowing costs. In response, Germany, France and the IMF have provided ad hoc bailouts through the European Financial Stability Facility (EFSF) in order to prevent a default that could undermine the Euro and lead to a broader crisis in the Eurozone. But despite receiving billions of Euros in aid, Greek 10 year bond yields remain high, indicating a low degree of investor confidence in Greece's long-term economic prospects.[5] This is partially due to the unpopularity of the austerity measures demanded by Germans in return for bailouts. The situation has deteriorated to the point where German and French leaders have started to openly discuss the possibility of an orderly default, in recognition that Greece is too deeply in debt to ever pay back investors. The lack of central control over fiscal policy has led to disparate responses to the crisis. The wealthy countries of the north do not want to burden their citizens with supranationalizing the debt through the extensive use of Eurobonds, nor do they want to lower the debt burdens through inflationary policies. Thus, growth remains anaemic and periodic bailouts remain the orthodox policy due to the institutional limitations of the Euro.

To compound the problems, a variety of nationalist movements across Europe have gained popularity. Countries like Austria, Hungary and Poland have experienced a dramatic increase in the support for parties that promote nationalist or neo-fascist agendas. Even in France—a country at the hub of the European project—support for the National Front has increased both due the economic problems associated with the Great Recession and domestic racial tensions along with terrorist attacks. Similarly, in Britain, the Conservatives party made a promise to hold a referendum on its continued role in the European Union as a method to appease supporters of the United Kingdom Independence Party (UKIP). When the referendum was held, the exit side narrowly pulled off a victory and will have to negotiate some form of an exit from the EU. While Britain has a history of Euroscepticism, this trend appears to be occurring across Europe, undermining the EU's unity and capabilities should another economic crisis occur.

The next chapter will continue by discussing the role of China. Although out of all the major regions China appears to have come out of the recession with few economic problems, underlying a seemingly assertive China is a self-conscious regime and a highly corrupt political and economic system. China has gone through 30 years of integration into the international economic system. It is now a hub of low-cost manufacturing for American companies. Many were expecting the recession to be the start of a newly assertive China emerging on the international scene. Indeed, it seemed the twenty-first century would belong to China. However, the regime has only participated in incremental domestic and international reforms. The central issue limiting China's advance is demographic. The regime must keep economic growth for fear a legitimacy crisis due to poor economic growth. The Chinese economy must absorb 30 million new workers every year into its major cities. Also, leading up to the recession China's relatively poor social security system means workers save a large portion of their income, leading to lower global interest rates. These factors prevent China from undergoing substantive economic reforms. It has to keep investing in American debt for fear that lower American consumption will negatively impact Chinese job growth. The nearly two trillion of debt owned by China has limited its policy options. If it tries to sell off its assets slowly, it will undermine confidence in the remaining US debt the Chinese government holds. Furthermore, any major recession in the USA will lower American consumption of Chinese-made goods. China's financial system and labour market is now dependent on US growth and economic stability.

Moreover, despite considerable improvements in living standards, China remains a poor country that must grapple with a range of domestic and regional challenges before it can hope to compete with America for pre-eminence. Yet again, China's difficulties are mainly demographic. Even after two decades of exponential growth, the Chinese economy is still less than one-third of the size of its American counterpart,[6] despite the fact that China's population is over four times larger than that of the USA. In China, domestic challenges have taken the form of a series of social pathologies that include rampant inequality, a greying population and an unbalanced gender ratio. Even though China has had an impressive level of economic growth in recent years, it must be kept in mind that, despite its growing prosperity, it is still a very poor country. Much of the population has been untouched by its rapid economic development. The bulk of China's workforce remains poor, especially in the countryside. In fact, the high level of economic inequality between rural and urban workers has led to concern that the Chinese economy is becoming "Latin Americanized", or extremely economically unequal.

Given the depth of these problems, it is unclear whether the government has the political or economic resources to deal with any or all of these issues.

Chapter 6 will change pace and build upon the earlier chapters by examining the response to the recession and the political polarization in the USA. I will provide an account of America's government structure and political culture. I will also discuss how its foreign policy has been motivated by both geopolitical threats and the interests of corporations and financial institutions. With the rise of neoliberalism in the 1970s, financial markets and corporations emerged as a major transnational force in the international system that overcame the boundaries and regulatory limitations of most nation-states. Most of the time, the relationship between the US government and global finance has been cooperative. In the 1980s and 1990s, the American government often yielded to the demands of finance capital by providing bailouts to prevent a broader systemic crisis in capitalism.

This chapter will continue the discussion of the American reaction to the terrorist attacks of September 11th, 2001, the resulting wars in Iraq and Afghanistan, and the after effects of the 2008 financial crisis. There were tensions between the American state, corporations, and financial markets due to the war in Iraq and the financial crisis. The subsequent Great Recession of the late 2000s was experienced differently in the USA, the EU and China due to the unevenness of the global capitalist system. Initially, President Barack Obama brought the promise of substantial change in the USA from the previous administration of George W. Bush. Yet very little has changed. The Obama Administration did not substantially regulated finance capital—if it is even possible for a single state to do so—nor has he radically altered US military policy in the Middle East and other regions. Global finance has shown throughout the global economy that it has the ability to condition the response of countries, punishing those that act contrary to the demands of investors.

While it is too soon to see the long-term economic ramifications of the recession on the USA, this crisis does show that America is under many constraints and suffers limitations due to its political system. America can benefit from the development international capitalism, particularly in the financialization of the system, but it can also be punished by financial markets. In the post 2008 election, the Democrats had control of the Whitehouse and Congress. Although Obama passed a bailout package, both Republican opposition and the Tea Party began to limit the policy options available. In the wake of 2010 midterms, the Republicans are in control the House of Representatives, with a sizable portion of the caucus part of the Tea Party. The opposition from the House has prevented major policy initiatives from the Obama administration. Republican opposition has almost led to another global financial crisis. In the summer of 2011, the USA nearly went into default on its debt, due to the inability of the government to agree to raise the debt ceiling. This chapter will highlight the polarization of the American political system as the main reason reform of the financial system is unlikely to be substantive. It will also discuss the subsequent rise of Republican presidential candidate Donald Trump and the right-wing populist backlash against the Republican and Democratic establishment. Rather than a political exception, Trump represents a rejection of America's role as hegemon and the USAs' continued support for the very institutions that are the cornerstone of the international world order.

The final chapter will discuss the consequences of inaction, polarization and anger by providing a series of prescriptions. The liberalization of the financial system has led to a protracted economic crisis in America and the Eurozone, and even China's economic system shows signs of troubles. Despite some stability in the global economy, the recovery remains fragile and any number of issues could lead to another crisis. Political polarization in the USA could lead to series of bank failures, or America could simply default on its debt, leading to a global economic catastrophe. Trump's presidency could undermine long-standing institutions, like NAFTA and NATO. The Eurozone is far from stable—a sovereign default of Italy or Spain could have far-reaching consequences. As well, China's economic system is rife with corruption and favouritism. There have been widespread fears of a housing bubble in major cities that could undermine China's economic growth and political stability. Any of these issues, or indeed all of them, could jeopardize the stability of the global economy and make a protracted economic slump into a much longer and more serious depression.

This, however, does not have to be the case. There are reforms that could be undertaken—some simple others more serious—that could prevent another crisis from occurring. In the USA, political reforms of its electoral system and the regulation of campaign finance could lessen the effects of polarization. A US government not limited by factional infighting could provide leadership to reform its financial sector and potentially global economic system. In Europe, countries either have to supranationalize, providing more fiscal authority to the EU or radically reform the member-states tied to the Euro. As is, the forced austerity measures as part of the conditions for periodic bailouts are having deleterious effects on both the economies of Europe's south and their political stability. China's demographic problems are more structural and difficult from a policy perspective, but the negative effects of can be ameliorated. First, its economy needs further reform. The nexus between state-owned enterprises and the Communist Party has led to widespread corruption, there needs to be a clearer separation between business and the government. Also, China's government could provide more services to the poor though changes to its social insurance system. Although it would be expensive, it would lessen the discrepancy between rich and power and lower the savings rate since many in China have to provide for their old age and medical bills. Obviously some political reform would be desirable, but as of yet, it remains improbable compared to other, more readily achievable policies.

There are several overall goals for this book. First, my work will contribute to a growing body of the literature on the Great Recession. However, where this book differs is that it offers a broader examination of the crisis. My examination will not just look at institutions, but on the politics that can either challenge or underwrite the very institutions that keep global order. Also, I will examine the complex intersections of a variety of approaches. I will appropriate the critical literature to examine the global economy as a whole, but from there I will delve into the literature on polarization to evaluate the American case, the institutional literature for the Eurozone and work on demographics in China. Capitalism is a decentralized system of accumulation that breaks down spatial and political boundaries in search of profit, but along the way it has to deal with domestic, contingent factors.[7] So while it would be simpler to focus on the political apparatus or on the capitalist system, each side represents two interlinked determinants.

николаевниколаевNotes

1. Charles Kindleberger. *The World in Depression 1929–1939* (Berkeley: University of California Press, 1973): 2.
2. Bryan Mabee "Discourses of Empire: The US 'Empire', Globalisation and International Relations". *Third World Quarterly*, Vol. 25, No. 8 (2004): 1361.
3. Ibid., 118.
4. The Economist, "The euro area's debt crisis", *The Economist*. (12 January 2011): http://www.economist.com/node/17902709.

5. BBC Business News, "Euro falls on rumours Greece is to quit the Eurozone", *BBC News Magazine* (7 May 2011): http://www.bbc.co.uk/news/business-13317770.
6. The World Bank estimates China's nominal GDP at $4.5 trillion, making it a fraction of America's $14.1 trillion annual output, CIA Worldfactbook, Country Comparison: GDP—per capita (PPP), *Central Intelligence Agency*. Washington, D.C. (July 2010): https://www.cia.gov/library/publications/the-world-factbook/rankorder/2004rank.html?countryName=China&countryCode=ch&regionCode=eas&rank=126#ch.
7. David Harvey. *Limits to Capital* (London; New York: Verso, 2006).

CHAPTER 2

The Great Wars and the Post-war Consensus 1914–1979

Throughout the twentieth century, there have been contradictions in capitalism that have reached the point of crisis. This chapter will examine the historical determinants behind the Great Depression in the 1930s, the period of stagflation during the 1970s and the Great Recession that began in 2008. This chapter will set the stage by discussing the foundations of American hegemony and the establishment and collapse of the Bretton Woods system of finance. It will begin by discussing the economic and political chaos of the post-WWI era. A remarkable feature of the time was the political unwillingness of the USA to play a key role in European affairs, particularly in the League of Nations after the First World War. The failures of the interwar years are many: a global depression and the failure of the USA and European powers to prevent another catastrophic global conflict. In the wake of the worst war in human history, the USA along with its allies forged a new economic and political order—the Bretton Woods system which regulated the flows of finance and promoted free trade and open markets. However, as I will elaborate upon in greater detail by the late 1960s, contradictions began to arise in the post-war consensus. By the 1970s, the Bretton Woods system began to be dismantled by the USA before being fully rejected in the Reagan-Thatcher era. This chapter will conclude just prior to election of Margaret Thatcher in Britain 1979 and Ronald Reagan as US President in 1980 and the ramifications of their election will be explored in more detail in Chap. 3.

A goal of these next two chapters is to show how events cannot be abstracted from their historical and social context. For example, the

© The Author(s) 2018
B. Tozzo, *American Hegemony after the Great Recession*, International Political Economy Series, https://doi.org/10.1057/978-1-137-57539-5_2

recent recession has far-reaching historical roots, dating back to policy decisions made by President Roosevelt during the 1930s. Although these chapters place emphasis on the USA, they will also discuss transformations in the broader global system. I will examine how changes in capitalism can, at times, emerge gradually before leading to a broader transformation in the entire system, most recently evident in the rise of neoliberalism in the late 1970s and early 1980s. Although neoliberalism is often attributed to the policies of Margaret Thatcher and Ronald Reagan, as I will show, quantitative changes had begun to occur by the late 1960s in the capitalist system, leading to experimentation in places like Chile. The qualitative global transformation to neoliberalism did not occur suddenly, but took nearly 20 years to become orthodox in most Western countries. Even still, there remains a great deal of tension both within and between governments over economic policy and distribution.

Technological changes also had an impact on the political and social changes that occurred due to major innovations in production and finance, such as air transportation technology and the Internet. At the same time, these innovations are not always progressive, but can lead to new forms of opposition in the system, such as global terrorist networks like Al-Qaeda. These technological advances have linked governments and economies together at a historically unprecedented level. Furthermore, a fundamental methodological distinction of this analysis is its focus on determinants rather than absolute causes of processes. It avoids generalizations that abstract phenomena from their history and context and will discuss concepts as open-ended, requiring contextualization to understand their meaning.

Lessons from the Great Depression

This section will outline the contradiction in capitalism that occurred in the 1930s, and the inadequate response of the USA to manage the ensuing crisis. This was a period of a high degree of international instability due to the recent experience of the First World War. Although the USA was a major economic power, it had not yet become the hegemon of the capitalist system, but instead had an ad hoc role in managing periodic economic and political crises. Also European countries had become reliant on American loans to ensure their economic stability. Without financing from the USA, the German government was unable to pay its reparations. When the crisis hit, the reluctance of Washington to properly mitigate the crisis, the limitations of the gold standard, as well as an already weakened global economy led to a decade-long depression.

One of the determining factors of the depression was the inability of a potentially hegemonic country, the USA, to organize a coordinated response to a crisis in capitalism. The "victors" of the First World War, France and Britain, were economically bankrupt having spent most of their resources fighting the Central Powers.[1] Moreover, the war left Russia in the middle of a civil war. Two defeated empires, Austria-Hungary and the Ottoman Empire, were partitioned along national lines into a series of new countries. For the Germans, the Treaty of Versailles required financial reparation payments (although under relatively flexible terms), as well as recognition that the Central Powers caused the conflict.[2] The only state that could reorganize the system and take a hegemonic position was the USA. Due to the massive costs of the First World War for Britain, America had become the international financial hub of the global economy as well as its main lender.[3] The USA had the potential to take over the role of Britain as hegemon of the capitalist system. Germany defaulted on repaying its reparations in 1924 leading to hyperinflation. In response, Washington took a leadership role providing loans through the Dawes Plan. Republicans in the USA were sceptical about intervening in European affairs, having previously prevented America's entrance into the League of Nations. However, the economic hardship in the heart of Europe, the Americans provided access to financial assets so that Germany could repay its debts to Britain and France, which helped alleviate postwar tensions. This had two significant economic and political implications for the interwar years: it provided the Germans a period of stability, and it made European prosperity dependent upon the American economy. Thus, when the USA entered a period of crisis in 1929, it had repercussions throughout Europe and the global economy.

In the 1920s, there was a large amount of speculation on Wall Street as many Americans borrowed money in order to invest in the booming stock market. By 1928, the American Federal Reserve recognized that the stock market was crowding out investment in other productive areas and decided to raise interest rates to stem bank loans.[4] In October 1929, the speculative bubble burst. In two days, the stock market lost nearly 30% of its value.[5] Many investors could no longer repay their bank loans due to the abrupt decline. But rather than a minor downturn, the stock market did not rebound to its pre-1929 level until the early 1950s.[6] Banks were over-leveraged due to the generous loans they provided, partially to the German government, and could not pay back their deposits.[7] This resulted in a series of bank runs throughout the USA as citizens worried their savings would be lost due to the collapsing banking system. The liquidity crunch made it difficult for both businesses and individuals to obtain loans, leading to a dramatic decline in employment as the demand for goods and agricultural products collapsed.[8] Unemployment increased dramatically from 3% in 1929 to 25% by the end of 1930.[9] With the entire American economy on the verge of collapse, the US government under the Republican Herbert Hoover started to intervene in order to alleviate the crisis.

However, the policies of the American government worsened an already precarious economic situation. In response to the banking crisis, the Federal Reserve cut interest rates, but this proved to be an inadequate measure to stem bank failures.[10] The banking system was already far too weakened for a reduction of interest rates alone to resolve the crisis. In 1930 and 1931, the American government could not prevent them from failing, with over 900 banks closing in total at a loss of billions of dollars of deposits.[11] The problem became cyclical: as banks failed, people lost their faith in the financial system, and as people were no longer willing to deposit in banks the situation further deteriorated. Moreover, federal government spending remained constant—there was no fiscal stimulus in order to counteract the collapse in demand and purchasing power, nor bailouts of major financial institutions.[12] To make the situation even worse, in 1930, Congress enacted a series of taxes on imported goods with the Smoot-Hawley Tariff Act.[13] This was intended to bolster the domestic market, but the tariffs closed off markets for American exports as countries retaliated by increasing their own tariffs. Both as a result of the collapse in demand and new tariffs, world trade collapsed from $5.3 billion in 1929 to $1.3 billion by 1933 (figures in 1933 US dollars).[14] The failure of the Federal Reserve and the US government to respond appropriately to the crisis led a downturn on Wall Street to become a widespread global depression.

Another major determinant of the depression was the gold standard, which proved to be a major constraint on government spending. The inflation that followed the First World War led France, the USA, Germany and the UK to return to the gold in order to provide financial stability.[15] Germany in particular had experienced a period of hyperinflation after the First World War due to the inability of its government to pay its war reparations. By fixing the value of a currency to gold, the system heavily restricted the growth in the money supply by allowing domestic and foreign investors to transfer their money to gold.[16] During the interwar years, investors had the ability to undermine a country's financial system if a government tried to devalue its currency or undertook long-term deficit spending. The gold standard led to competition between countries as investors could easily move their assets due to the international acceptance of gold.[17] After the Wall Street crash and subsequent bank failures, the gold standard ended up being a major contributor to deflation. It prevented governments from injecting liquidity in order to prevent bank failures or using protracted deficit spending in order to shore up demand. But more importantly, the gold standard prevented governments from coordinating economic policy and contributed to rising international tension brought on by the depression.

The gold standard proved to be significant—it restricted governments intervention in the economy and a determinant of the depression. By the late 1920s, there had been a substantial increase in economic inequality in the USA. After the war, it became politically difficult to tax the wealthy, and the gold standard made it impossible for countries to engage in deficit spending to promote economic equality. By 1929, the top 1% owned 30% of all household wealth, a level that was not reached again until the 1990s.[18] Unlike Britain during the pre-war period, the US government refused to take a leadership role to coordinate countries to alleviate the depression. The USA undermined economic cooperation by introducing tariffs in order to protect domestic industries. America's trading partners responded by enacting a series of "beggar-thy-neighbour" policies to promote their own industries, undermining global free trade and global economic growth. Internationally, America was willing to finance loans to Europe as long as its own economy was growing, but when the depression hit the entire system collapsed. The Germans depended upon American financing in order to finance their post-WWI reparation payments through the Dawes Plan.[19] By cutting off the money, the crisis to Europe. In Germany, this led to a massive economic depression with unemployment reaching over 25% and GDP contracting by nearly 30% by 1932.[20] The depression fuelled the rise of radicalism throughout the West and contributed to the rise of Adolf Hitler's Nazi Party to power in 1933.

In the USA, the depression led to the election of Franklin Roosevelt in 1932 with the support of labour unions, farmers, Southern whites and minorities. Roosevelt promised to reinvigorate the economy and provide relief for the unemployed. His administration began the New Deal which introduced a series of social programs and industrial planning through the National Recovery Act, and the Wagner Act which promoted unionization.[21] Roosevelt was sympathetic to the plight of the working class and the poor. However, his administration faced opposition from corporate and financial interests:

> the growth of (noncompany) unions threatened capitalist prerogatives in the workplace, and the disproportionate expansion of industrial as opposed to craft unions united broader sectors of industrial labour than at any previous period in U.S. history. Capitalists (with very few exceptions) regarded all of this as threatening and believed that the federal government was encouraging labour… whose results were not fully predictable or necessarily controllable.[22]

American investors and corporate owners were worried about the amount of power unions gained from Roosevelt's government, fearing that it would undermine profitability and challenge private property. Under Roosevelt's tenure, unions took an unprecedented amount of power in collective bargaining. Furthermore, the social programs introduced by Roosevelt expanded the role of government in the economy, providing old-age pensions, unemployment relief, infrastructure projects, and farm subsidies.[23] The federal government tried to combat the deflationary spiral of the Great Depression through job creation programs. Despite the opposition from a variety of capitalists, Roosevelt began to reorganize the American economy in order to decrease economic inequality and lower unemployment through the creation of a welfare system.

Much to the disappointment of domestic and international financiers, Congress passed legislation to regulate the American financial system. In order to prevent further bankruptcies, the Glass-Steagall Act of 1933 was signed into law. The act founded the Federal Deposit Insurance Corporation (FDIC)—this was intended to return confidence to the banking system through a government guarantee that deposits would be safe.[24] More consequentially, the Act put in place a firm legal barrier between commercial and investment banking.[25] Commercial banks were restricted to day-to-day banking, small loans and mortgages while investment banks could trade stocks and bonds. The general purpose was to limit the exposure of people's savings—now insured by the government—from the fluctuations of the stock market.[26] It prevented bankers from using higher interest rates to attract deposits, and then using that money to invest in risky business ventures. Roosevelt also started to introduce incentives to increase home ownership by insuring mortgages for people with low down payments (though this program was only available to whites), which was later turned into a formal institution the Federal National Mortgage Association or Fannie Mae.[27] Roosevelt's reforms meant nearly every aspect of the financial system had some form of government oversight, whether in the form of insurance or regulation. In order to enforce these regulations, the federal government established the Securities and Exchange Commission (SEC) to ensure that corporations followed the new laws to give accurate information to investors. The overall aim of the new legislation was to prevent problems related to the Great Depression from recurring and to restore confidence in the economy.

Many industrialists and investors worried that capitalism itself would soon be threatened by the "radical" reforms of the Roosevelt administration.[28] Initially, the New Deal was met with resentment from moneyed interests in America, to the point of tentatively plotting his overthrow in a failed coup attempt to replace the president with Major General Smedley Butler.[29] Yet Roosevelt was far from a revolutionary even by the standards of the era. Countries throughout Europe were becoming even more extreme, either adopting fascism or communism. Roosevelt's New Deal was a reformist attempt to preserve and regulate American capitalism in order to save the system by preventing the radicalization of the working class and the poor. Regardless of the policies that empowered the working class, Roosevelt was still constrained by the American political and economic system. During the early phases of the New Deal, the Supreme Court ruled that several programs, such as the National Recovery Act, were unconstitutional, and after 1938 a conservative coalition of Republicans and Democrats held the majority of seats in Congress.[30] Moreover, due to the inability of the USA to coordinate with Britain and France, even the widespread abandonment of the gold standard between 1933 and 1936 did little to strengthen the global economy.[31] Roosevelt's financial reforms were intended to return confidence to the free market rather than alter its role. Though the New Deal may have seemed radical by the standards of the USA in the 1930s, Roosevelt's policies offered only incremental change to deal with the economic hardships brought on by the Great Depression.

In the area of fiscal policy, the New Deal did not offer the stimulus required to deal with unemployment or to stabilize the financial system. In 1932, Roosevelt had campaigned calling for "the one sound foundation of permanent economic recovery—a complete and honest balancing of the federal budget".[32] A return to balanced budgets was orthodox thinking at the time. Roosevelt's administration was reluctant to increase taxes on the wealthy in order to pay for wider economic distribution, which limited government spending and redistribution efforts.[33] Roosevelt became president 3 years before Keynes' views were popularized in *The General Theory of Employment, Interest and Money*. Keynes argued governments must produce deficits in times of hardship in order to boost aggregate demand to return the economy to full employment.[34] Once in office Roosevelt introduced several new social programs, but the federal debt remained constant throughout the 1930s at around 40% of GNP.[35] This brought down unemployment, but it still remained high compared to the pre-depression era. The New Deal pushed unemployment down from its height of 25% in 1933 to 15% in 1937.[36] Even these policies were hampered by the conservative coalition elected in the 1938 midterms whose austerity measures pushed the jobless rate back to 19% by 1939.[37] It would take the Second World War before the USA returned to full employment.

The inability of the USA to take a leadership role to mitigate the economic crisis of the Great Depression led to a global depression and the outbreak of the Second World War. Prior to the First World War, Britain coordinated the global economy, acting as hegemon. With its empire fragmenting and the country bankrupt, the UK did not have the political will or economic ability to foster the international consensus required to prevent another global conflict.[38] The only country that had the economic strength to underwrite the international financial system in the interwar period was the USA. It did so intermittently in the 1920s and failed completely to react to the emerging crisis is capitalism in the 1930s. In 1933, there was an international conference held to find consensus to deal with the crisis by regulating currency exchanges.[39] Rather than taking a leadership role, the American government acted as obstructionists, refusing to take part in any agreement, rendering the conference futile.[40] This was due to competing interests. America had the capability to act as the hegemon of the international system, but domestic political and economic interests coincided to prevent it from being the dominant country. The USA was far more concerned with its own short-term economic gain regardless of the consequences for the international community. With the prospects for profitability low and states closing off their economies to foreign trade, global capital investment ground to a halt, worsening an already dire situation.

The Great Depression of the 1930s was the result of a global reorganization of capitalism due to the First World War and a major speculative bubble in America. The USA, now central to the global economy, refused to coordinate a coherent response to the crisis, leading to a protracted depression in the global economy. There were several determinants of this lack of coordination. The first was due to the orthodox political thinking of the time—the American government tried to keep deficit spending low and only incrementally increased regulation of the economy. The second determinant was the way the monetary system was organized immediately after the First World War. Countries were worried about inflation and returned to the gold standard, thereby heavily constraining liquidity and reining in government spending. When Wall Street collapsed the gold standard proved to be a major barrier to government intervention and international cooperation. The historical legacy of American scepticism towards involvement in Europe led to "beggar-thy-neighbor" policies. By the late 1930s, Roosevelt began to recognize that America had to play a leadership role in international military, political and economic affairs. But by this time, the damage was done. It was far too late to avert the Second World War.

THE POST-WWII AMERICAN NEW ORDER

After the Second World War, America was in an unprecedented superior position vis-a-via the other former belligerents. Moreover, its leaders had the political will, due to international competition, to act as the hegemon of the capitalist system. The other remaining superpower, the Soviet Union, had lost millions of people in a war fought over its home territory. The two objectives would become the priority of the US government in the post-war period: to prevent the spread of communism in Europe and elsewhere and to open new markets by free trade. As the hegemon of the capitalist system, the US government worked to manage the capitalist system, intervening when the interests of investors and corporations were threatened. Yet the Americans were also compelled to prevent the expansion of the Soviet Union. The American government's fear of Communism led to the domestic rise of McCarthyism, as the government tried to eliminate subversive people in the media, academia and in government. These two features would be the main determinants of the post-war system: America had to prevent the sphere of influence of the Soviet Union, while, at the same time, promoting the expansion of capitalism. Although these two tasks were often complementary, as

I will discuss, there arose contradictions between the containment of Communism and the expansion of markets.

In order to prevent another catastrophic global depression and major international conflict, the USA along with Britain as a junior partner instituted an international regulatory regime. The agreement reached at Bretton Woods, New Hampshire (called the Bretton Woods system) regulated finance through the International Monetary Fund (IMF) by pegging currencies to the US dollar, which then could be exchanged for gold.[41] The system was intended to prevent massive currency fluctuations from speculators, yet still allows countries flexibility to devalue in case of a crisis. To further ease a balance of payment problem, the IMF provided short-term loans to countries and the International Bank of Reconstruction and Development (later the name was changed to the World Bark) was put in charge of rebuilding Europe.[42] Each of these institutions was put in place due to the experience of the depression. The goal was to ease the business cycle to produce full employment, to prevent countries from defaulting on their debt, and to lower tariff barriers to promote and expand free trade. The Americans were the undisputed hegemon in the capitalist system and the new global order reflected their values.

While trade barriers were to be lowered and Europe rebuilt, investment, capital and finance were to be highly regulated. As John Maynard Keynes stated "control of capital movements" would be a "permanent feature of the post war system".[43] To this end in 1947, many Western countries signed the General Agreement on Tariffs and Trade (GATT) which through a series of agreements liberalized trade and reduced tariff barriers. In response to the post-war devastation, the USA introduced the Marshall Plan to aid in the reconstruction of Europe. In 1951, in order to foster free trade and to prevent France and Germany from having sole ownership of the materials needed for war, the European Coal and Steel Community was adopted—a precursor to the European Union. The post-war period was one where America used its position to open markets through the use of incentives, both through international organizations and through aid. Due to the relative devastation of the rest of the world, America could dictate the shape of new international order. Trade became progressively liberalized, with America as a central producer, lender and consumer in the global capitalist system.

There had been a significant amount of technological development in the areas of medicine, industry, and in air and motor vehicles from Germany, the UK, France and the USA.[44] With the onset of the Second

World War, government had invested heavily in military technology and industrial infrastructure, with the USA winning the race to develop the first atomic bomb. Consequently, the technologies that were developed during the war ended up having numerous civilian applications, from producing relatively inexpensive automobiles to advances in air transportation and travel.[45] America's war experience left the country with control over most of the world's money and gold reserves. As Arrighi discusses:

> As a result of... its trade and current account surplus, the United States came to enjoy a virtual monopoly of world liquidity. In 1947, its gold reserves were 70 percent of the world's total. Moreover, the excess demand for dollars by foreign governments and businesses meant that US control over world liquidity was far greater than implied by this extraordinary concentration of monetary gold.[46]

By almost any measure, America was in the best position relative to the other allies. The war had left Europe in ruins. Britain was bankrupt, France had been occupied from 1940 to 1945 and the Soviet Union had lost nearly 30 million people due to the war. With its strong and productive industrial base, a plethora of new technologies, and its mass reserves of capital, the USA was in the unique historical position to dictate the terms of the post-war order. The USA began to govern the international economy according to its own preferences in order to rebuild Europe, prevent the spread of Communism and open markets to trade.

The rebuilding of Western Europe and Japan became of paramount importance for Washington. With the USSR an aggressive and expansionist superpower, there was an immediate need ensure the survival of capitalism in Germany, France, the UK and Japan. A result of American loans was an "economic miracle" in Germany and Japan. This was partially determined by macroeconomic factors such as access to the wealthy US consumer market, while maintaining a favourable exchange rate.[47] There was also a shift throughout Western countries towards consumer-oriented economies. Germany and Japan were also helped by domestic factors since both countries had access to a pool of highly educated and skilled labourers. A corporatist model of industrial organization brought capital and labour together in policy-making in Germany. In Japan, a system of worker patronage developed that guaranteed lifetime employment in order to ensure the loyalty of workers.[48] Indeed, the period from 1946 to 1971 was the pinnacle of the "historic compromise" between capital and labour in most developed countries.[49] Although trade was becoming increasingly free, foreign investment was highly regulated to prevent competition between countries for finance. Moreover, sectors of the economy in Western Europe and North America were nationalized in order to meet the demands of the public.[50] States provided more comprehensive social insurance programs, such as old-age pensions, universal health care and unemployment insurance—though this varied from country to country. It seemed that capitalism was becoming increasingly dominated by government intervention.

There were geopolitical reasons behind the USA replacing Britain as the dominant capitalist country after the Second World War. There was a threat from the Soviet Union which had occupied most of Eastern Europe and sought to increase its sphere of influence. Devastated by two world wars, Britain no longer had the financial and military capacity to ward off Soviet expansionism, which became apparent when America took over Britain's role in the Greek Civil War in 1946.[51] The USA alone had the military and economic resources to prevent the spread of international communism. Prior to the Second World War, the US government was reluctant to involve itself in European affairs. With the onset of the Cold War, the American military became necessary to protect financial and political interests against the Soviet Union. America formed an international defensive pact, the North Atlantic Treaty Organization (NATO), which formalized a protective military alliance with Western Europe against the Soviet Union. Also the United Nations was established as an intergovernmental institution committed to global peace and security. The USA had become the guarantor against Soviet expansion, contributing to proxy wars in Korea (1950–1954), Vietnam (1955–1975) and Afghanistan (1979–1989). While at the same time, the USA propped up regimes with military and foreign aid—at times unsuccessfully—in Cuba and later Iran. The policy of America and its allies was one of "containment" to prevent Soviet influence from spreading globally and undermining US economic and security interests.[52] Indeed, the Cold War conflict became one of the most prominent geopolitical features of the twentieth century, with the USA and USSR competing for allies, territory and spheres of control with nuclear war a constant threat.

During the Cold War, many countries instituted Marxist-Leninist state control of their economy, though not all the countries that did so allied with the Soviet Union. The world market was divided between free market economies and statist economies in the model of the USSR. Eastern Europe, many parts of the Middle East, China in 1947 and India in 1949 adopted central planning and state control of the economy—although India remained a democratic country. After the Second World War, the former Japanese colonies in Southeast Asia were divided between the allies, and the bankrupt British and French ended formal colonial rule of India and most African states.[53] Many countries followed the Soviet model of planned economies after they were decolonized by Britain and France. This formal decolonization and socialist central planning effectively limited the pool of global labour, closing off many countries from the global economy. Decolonization was a reflection of the American cultural aversion to formal empires as well as the decline in military and economic power in Britain and France. Although the USA often dictated the political regime's affiliation and economic system, and intervened only when its interests were threatened, it left day-to-day management to local elites.[54] Washington did not care if a regime was authoritarian, or even if it perpetuated human rights abuses, such as in Saudi Arabia or the Philippines, so long as it did not ally with the Soviet Union.

The Korean War was a major military conflict in the early part of the Cold War. Up until the end of the Second World War, Korea was a Japanese colony. After the war, it was partitioned along the 38th parallel between the Democratic People's Republic of Korea (DPRK) in the North, a regime installed by the Soviets, and the Republic of Korea (ROK) in the South a regime created by the Western allies. With each side committed to reunification, North Korea's leader Kim Il-Sung invaded the South after securing arms from the Soviet Union and personnel from the newly communist People's Republic of China (PRC).[55] The ROK was short on war materials and had poorly trained troops compared to the North Koreans who had fought in the Chinese civil war.[56] The South would have almost certainly lost if it did not have outside intervention from the USA. At the time, the American government had most of its energy and resources devoted to rebuilding Western Europe and did not want to devote the time nor military resources to preserve the ROK—the US Congress even defeated an aid package for South Korea in 1950.[57] Though pressure was placed on the American government to act, it was reluctant to get involved in Korea due to its own domestic politics. Eventually though, with the backing of the United Nations, the USA sent forces into Korea in order to prevent the peninsula unifying under the Communists. The war went on until a truce was signed in 1954 with Korea permanently divided between the North and South.

Although the USA recognized it had an economic and geopolitical interest in preventing the expansion of the Soviet Union in Europe, South Korea was a different situation altogether. There were few economic incentives to invest in South Korea for the USA. The Americans were reluctant to send forces to protect the ROK as the country was poor, politically unstable and had few natural resources.[58] Even losing the peninsula to communism was not, at first, important to Washington. However, once the USA realized there was foreign involvement supporting the DPRK, the need to counterbalance the Soviet Union was a major determining factor behind American intervention. If the USA did not get involved, the South would have been overrun by the well-trained and better-armed military of the DPRK. The intervention was not motivated by an accumulation strategy, in fact, quite the opposite, there were few direct profits to be made in the impoverished South Korea. It was the involvement of the Soviet Union and China that compelled the USA to send in its military. After the war, the Americans supported the regime in South Korea by placing troops along the 38th parallel and with military aid. The ROK government tried an import-substitution industrializing (ISI) strategy by placing tariffs on imports in order foster domestic industry. This policy failed and the Korean economy stagnated in the 1950s leading to a military coup in 1961—though the dictator Park Chung-hee was an ally of the USA.[59]

With nearly $4.2 billion in economic assistance to South Korea between 1952 and 1969, the Park government started to invest in industries that exported to the American market. The Koreans started with low-end goods, promoted strong successful national corporations, and eventually invested in heavy industry.[60] The pace of South Korea's economic development was impressive, moving to higher tech industries as wages and the standards of living increased throughout the 1970s.[61] Unlike other developing countries in much of Africa, the USA had a strategic reason to prevent South Korea from collapsing due to economic stagnation. It provided the ROK with aid to construct its domestic industries, allowed it to have protective barriers around key corporations, and access to the wealthy American consumer market. At the domestic level, the Park government provided the stability to build an industrial base. So though initially this was done for geopolitical reasons, South Korea eventually became an important provider of cheap labour and imports for the USA, integrating the country into the capitalist system.

American military dominance and the expansion of markets defined the post-war era, as the USA needed to expand markets as an accumulation strategy and to counterbalance the USSR. The immediate post-war period sought to limit the ability of finance to move between states, with a high degree of regulation and oversight. When foreign capital was invested, the American government protected it through the use of its military. Washington propped up regimes that were sympathetic to Western corporations. In the case of Cuba, American firms had had invested more than in any other Latin American country prior to the revolution.[62] The USA had invested over $2 billion (in 1959 figures) in Cuba in agriculture, mining and infrastructure.[63] This was a large sum of money in a country relatively close to the US mainland. When a revolution occurred in 1959 with Fidel Castro's communists overthrowing the regime in Cuba, the interests of American capital and the US government coincided. The Americans tried, but failed, to overthrow Castro during the Bay of Pigs invasion in 1961. The Cold War context constrained military options for the USA with Cuba. The USSR became a guarantor of Cuba's independence, even to nearly leading to all-out war during the Cuban Missile Crisis. Eventually, the USA brokered an agreement with the USSR that prevented an invasion of Cuba. The demands of capitalists came into conflict with the geopolitical tensions of the Cold War. Although there was an initial attempt to reconcile capital interests in Cuba, the possible retaliation from the USSR prevented a broader response from the USA.

Although the interests of American and British capitalists often coincided with the need to counterbalance the USSR, the war in Vietnam was a protracted conflict that was not exclusively determined by an accumulation strategy. Again the politics of the Cold War was a significant factor behind American military intervention. American intervention in Vietnam was a response to the expansionism of the Soviet Union. The economic motivations for expansion into Vietnam are less than compelling. Mainly, Vietnam produced agricultural products, particularly white rice[64]—hardly a vital economic resource for global production. Moreover, there were cheaper and better-skilled workers in the recently conquered Japan for Vietnam to be needed as a labour market. So while the material interests of capitalists may not have been the main determinant in this conflict, it is not that it was not a factor *at all*. Many American defence firms profited from the mass investment of the US government due to the conflict, as the government provided billions for arms and weapons.[65] The war provided money for the private military establishment in the USA, but there were also many indirect industries that profited from the war.[66] So it cannot be discounted the war in Vietnam benefited domestic industries, however, the US economy as a whole was not strengthened from the war as there were little profit to be made in Vietnam to American firms. In the 1960s, Vietnam was a poor agrarian country used mainly by the French for raw materials and minerals—hardly a motive for the US government to spend the $101 billion cost of fighting the Viet Cong ($680 billion in 2008 dollars).[67] A major reason for the length of war was geopolitical—as a proxy war against the Soviet Union.

Despite some firms and corporations profiting from the war in Vietnam, the protracted and expensive conflict was detrimental to the broader American economy. The low unemployment, liberal domestic monetary policies, and massive social and military spending led to inflation reaching 10.6% in the second half of 1966, and remained around 5% throughout the remainder of the 1960s.[68] Compared to the higher inflation rates in the 1970s, this may not appear to be problematic, but it was coupled with the decline of public support for the war in Vietnam. There were few economic and even fewer political reasons to continue the war in Vietnam outside of the Cold War context.[69] The conflict ended up costing Lyndon Johnson re-election in 1968 as he decided not to run for president again due to his unpopularity. In addition, the inflationary consequences of the war and the simultaneous attempt to conduct a domestic War on Poverty decreased the overall economic competitiveness of American industries. The government spent billions on the war at the cost of thousands of lives with little profit to show for the conflict. The Cold War was the main motivation behind the American involvement in Vietnam. The determinants for the conflict are not exclusively for the purposes of accumulation. In fact, quite the contrary, American foreign interventions may run counter to the demands of local and international capital. The economic consequences of the policies during the Vietnam conflict had significant implications for the USA and the global economic system.

In the post-World War II period, the USA constructed a Western economic and military order that sought to expand trade and markets while at the same time preventing the spread of communism. Washington needed to rebuild the economies in Western Europe and Japan to have markets to sell goods and fully entrench the ideals of a capitalist democratic order. This aligned with the goals of the military to prevent the spread of communism. Where American and Western economic interests were not threatened, such as in the case of Korea or Vietnam, there was an initial reluctance of the USA to commit resources to prevent their collapse. Once America committed its forces, as it continues to do in South Korea today and in Vietnam until the fall of Saigon, it becomes increasingly difficult to withdraw its troops. Even when there were tensions between the interests of capitalists and the government, international competition often led Americans to use the military to combat the Soviet threat in proxy wars. Panitch and Gindin[70] and David Harvey argue that markets must forcibly expand through the use of the US government in order to overcome the internal contradictions in capitalism. Certainly, this does characterize many conflicts during the Cold War, but this assumption downplays a key systemic pressure that shaped a large portion of America's foreign policy. The USA was involved in conflicts that had little foreseeable medium- or short-term economic gain. In the case of Vietnam, there was an abundance of cheap labour in Japan and Western Europe, and the incentive of capturing Vietnam's rice fields is uncompelling as necessary to the expansion of capitalism in comparison with the expense of the conflict. Washington's commitment of resources in the long run ended up harming the American economy.

The history of American involvement in Vietnam suggests capitalism is not the sole driving force behind the conflicts. This implies the two processes were interrelated in the post-war system but vary in degree, time and place. American foreign policy shifted as the geopolitical and economic demands of capitalism changed. American antipathy towards communism and radical labour movements influenced its dealings with Stalin and Mao. During the 1950s, the red scare led many to fear communists had infiltrated the US government, businesses and the entertainment industry. This was based on recent experiences with the Soviet Union: it had stolen plans to produce their own nuclear weapon and was supporting communist parties throughout the world. The anti-Soviet rhetoric was also a useful method to divide the world between those that aligned with the Western capitalist order and those that did not.

From the post-war period until the early 1970s, the system of regulated finance, free trade, consumerism and rising wages paved the way for long period of widespread sustained economic growth in the West. The American-led economic system was extremely successful in rebuilding Western Europe and Japan after the Second World War. Capital was able to find profit in new consumer economies in Europe and South Asia, while at the same time, wages and union movements gained strength. Due to the geopolitical and economic threat of communism, the USA constructed a post-war Western order against the Soviet Union. The USSR posed an existential threat to the West and acted to counter the expansion of the USA and global capitalism. In the 1960s, however, the burden of fighting a proxy war in Vietnam along with the increased foreign competition led the USA to begin to undermine the regulatory framework that underscored the global economy. As I will discuss in the next section, these domestic and international barriers to capitalism began to falter, and along with a prolonged period of economic crisis in the 1970s, created an economic, political and ideational shift that led to the emergence of neoliberalism.

The 1970s: The Beginning of the Shift to Neoliberalism

The 1970s marked the beginning of the end of the post-World War II system of embedded liberalism.[71] Liberalized finance was the norm prior to First World War, with international finance largely mobile, unregulated, and driven by market demands.[72] The interwar years and the Great Depression were decades of economic chaos, with rising tariff barriers and global finance grinding to a halt.[73] Financial markets during the immediate post-WWII period were regulated for the most part. But in the late 1960s, various contradictions began to break down the barriers put in place to prevent the free flows in finance. The system started to fracture in the hub of the international capitalist system: the USA. Out of slight quantitative changes that occurred in the 1960s and 1970s in the USA, emerged a new economic order—a qualitative transformation of the entire global economy. Indeed, it was America's rejection of embedded liberalism that launched the deregulation of finance. America tried to manage this crisis by lowering the economic and political barriers put in place to restrain financial capital. At times these barriers were gradually reduced, while at other times it was done forcefully, allowing for the re-emergence of the power of finance on a global scale. As I will discuss, the transition to neoliberalism was partially determined by transformations in information and communication technologies that made it possible for capital to flow across borders with greater ease at lower costs.[74] The ideas of Hayek about the reduced role of the state had been around since the 1930s and 1940s, yet they became prominent in the late 1970s due to the economic problems faced by Western countries. So although this new technology allowed money to move around the world with fewer restrictions, it was one of several significant determinants that began in the 1970s that led to the neoliberal shift.

The contradictions in the post-war order started to appear as America began to lose its economic competitiveness. The post-war economic system proved to be extremely successful in rebuilding the economies in Western Europe and Japan. As these countries regained their economic competitiveness, American goods could no longer dominate the market, nor could the US dollar be easily devalued due to its transferability to gold. The post-WWII system to rebuild Europe worked incredibly well, with West Germany becoming a major economic power. Believing the USA unable to limit its deficits, West Germany and France started to convert their reserves into gold undermining the American dollar's place in the system. Moreover, under Lyndon Johnson, the USA initiated the "Great Society" programs, while, at the same time, pouring resources into the expensive Vietnam War. The American economy started to experience 5% inflation per year, with the Nixon administration imposing wage and price controls in the early 1970s.[75] Due to inflation, American corporations further lost a competitive edge to Europeans and the Japanese. Furthermore, the American economy had trouble attracting investment capital due to regulations on foreign investment. One of the major consequences of the post-war years was the transfer of money from public control and oversight to private firms. Washington started to lose control of capital as investment moved to companies in Western Europe.[76] As private capital increased in European firms, it was often outside the American regulatory framework. For example, both Petrodollars and Eurodollars were inaccessible to the American economy due to restrictions on the movement of finance.[77]

There were a series of international and domestic problems at the end of the 1960s that led the American government to withdraw from the system of capital controls. In 1971, the Nixon administration decided to unilaterally end the US dollar's convertibility to gold as a method to regain America's competitiveness. In the early 1970s, the USA had to contend with both a budget and balance of trade deficit.[78] The dollar's convertibility allowed governments to trade their cash reserves should America face a prolonged period of economic instability. Unlike the contemporary period, the dollar's convertibility and capital controls made American deficit financing difficult and harmful to the overall economy. Though the USA was not the first country to float its currency—West Germany did so in 1971—but when America did so, it undermined the entire system. Nixon's decision was a method to attract capital and to regain the competitiveness the USA had lost. By 1973, most developed countries had floated their currencies; this was quickly followed by a flurry of "competitive deregulation" of the financial system in order to attract money.[79] The barriers put in place after the Second World War for finance were taken apart as each country competed for investment. Since finance could flow anywhere unimpeded by oversight from government, there was an incentive to make domestic economies attractive for international investment. Capital could move with increasingly fewer restrictions, and with advances in communication technology it could rapidly leave a country creating a panic—this would be a key feature in the global economy after the abandonment of the system of currency and capital controls.

The US government left the regulatory regime it was central to establishing and maintaining. The decision to abandon the dollar standard was intended to increase the competitiveness of the USA by lowering the value of its dollar. With fewer regulations, the Americans could attract foreign capital from Europe and the Middle East.[80] The decision from the Nixon administration was effective in strengthening the American economy in the short-term. As expected, foreign capital invested heavily in the USA, leading to an increased demand for American goods.[81] By 1973, America's current account deficit had largely been eliminated as European currencies strengthened against the dollar.[82] Moreover, suspending convertibility launched a series of industries that specialized in foreign investment, risk management, futures and currency speculation.[83] Since currencies could fluctuate in a single day, these industries worked to hedge against the risk in order to mitigate market volatility. In 1972, the International Money Market (IMM) opened, trading futures contracts on numerous currencies, such as the US dollar, the peso and the yen.[84] These industries provided financial firms a powerful voice over the economic policies of the state, threatening investor retaliation should policies be unfavourable to the interests of capital. The financial industry became even more important as countries progressively reduced capital controls and foreign investment regulations in the 1980s.[85] But more importantly, the era of institutional cooperation and coordination on currencies came to an end, as states competed against each other for investment. Although the USA retained its position as the central economy in the global system for the time being, the market could penalize countries that deviated from the demands of international finance. In effect, financial markets had started to return to the international economic system and began to restrict the ability to national governments to regulate their economies.

If the floating of currencies started the transition towards neoliberalism, it was aided by the economic turbulence in the 1970s. From the mid-1970s to the early 1980s, the USA went through a period of stagflation—high unemployment with high inflation. Though the causes of stagflation are widely contested and poorly understood, one of the main determinants was the oil embargoes of 1973 and 1979. The oil embargo from the Organization of the Petroleum Exporting Countries (OPEC) was a response to America's support of Israel in the Yom Kippur War.[86] After Israel was invaded by Syria and Egypt in October of 1973, the USA supplied the Israeli army with weapons. In response, the OPEC cut off oil supplies to countries that supported Israel. By the 1970s, the American economy had become increasingly dependent upon cheap imported oil from the Middle East. Due to the embargo, global energy prices tripled and immediately led to a recession that lasted until 1975.[87] Though inflation in the USA had already reached 5% by the late 1960s, the decreased supply of oil led to a price increase in almost every major sector of the international economy, pushing inflation as high as 10% by 1975.[88] By the second oil shock of 1979 that followed the Iranian revolution, the American economy had already experienced a decade of high unemployment and high inflation.[89] The overthrow of the Shah led to another embargo against the USA, leading to yet another energy crisis in the USA.[90] Along with the embarrassing Iranian hostage situation, the prolonged period of economic stagnation led many to start to challenge the orthodoxy of the post-war consensus.

Another determinant of inflation was the power of labour movements. Labour unions were capable of gaining higher wages, more benefits, and greater regulation in the workplace.[91] The strength of labour in the 1960s and 1970s led to increased production costs and the scope of the welfare state, undermining American competitiveness in the face of foreign competition.[92] By the late 1960s and early 1970s, unions began to strike with greater frequency and militancy, demanding higher wages and better working conditions.[93] As the economic situation started to worsen through the 1970s workers became more militant in their aims.[94] The success of labour unions contributed to inflationary pressures in the 1970s by driving up prices to pay for better wages and benefits. The restrictions on foreign investment made it difficult for capital to invest in low-wage countries; profits began to decline as American labour drove up the cost of production.[95] The post-war accumulation strategy in the USA was based upon a consensus between labour and capital to share the outcome of economic growth. This relied upon profitability, which was threatened by the strength of unions, the supply shock of two oil crises, competition from Europe and Japan, and the problems associated with prolonged inflation.

By floating the US dollar to overcome one contradiction in capital, Nixon started a long-term process of continual financial deregulation that fundamentally undermined the post-war economic order. Though it may have started by the abandonment of the gold standard to regain American competitiveness, it had unforeseen consequences for both the American and global economy. Financialization may have been a method to prolong American hegemony, but by the 1980s, the financial industry began to more assertively shape the policies of the US government. The energy crisis led to almost 10 years of high unemployment and inflation in America. Profitability was threatened, and it seemed that the Keynesian policies of government intervention and regulation could no longer ensure high standards of living. In response to the inability of governments to adequately deal these economic problems, by the late 1970s and early 1980s, countries throughout the developed world elected politicians that promised a return to prosperity through reactionary economic and political platforms.

Neoliberalism Comes of Age

Though the election of Margaret Thatcher in Britain in 1979 and Ronald Reagan in 1980 is often viewed as the start of neoliberalism as a political force, the transition was already well under way by that time. Nevertheless, it was during the 1980s that the globalization of finance became a dominant process in the global economy. Reagan and Thatcher argued government intervention was the cause of the economic problems of the 1970s and that a reduction in public spending would lead to prosperity. They believed in the economic philosophies of Fredrick Von Hayek and Milton Friedman where the market would be guided by supply and demand.[96] While the politics of the Reagan administration were important in ending embedded liberalism, it was not the only determining factor that led to the onset of neoliberalism. There were technological and political shifts that led to the opening of large pools of cheap labour in China the 1980s and later India in the 1990s. Moreover, innovations in shipping and communications technology became cheaper allowing for greater outsourcing, leading to just-in-time inventory control systems and international production chains. There were broader systemic changes in the global economy that occurred along with neoliberal policies being instituted throughout the West.

The US government instituted a series of policies to weaken the power of unions and retrench the welfare state in order to make the business climate more favourable for investors. This initiated a process that would become commonplace: the government would deregulate or privatize a sector of the economy, private financiers would invest heavily, then its value would collapse requiring public money to prevent a broader crisis. Although Reagan and Thatcher are often viewed as the catalysts for deregulation and "the return of the market", it was first tried in South America. The "success" of these policies spread throughout the West in the 1980s and led to an expansion of the wealth of financiers and investors at the expense of the public and labour. By the 1990s, neoliberalism would become the new orthodoxy for left- and right-wing parties through the developed world.

The first significant post-war experiments with neoliberalism were under the rule of the Chilean dictator Augusto Pinochet. In the 1970 election, Salvador Allende of the Socialist Party led the "Popular Unity" coalition of socialists, communists and social democrats to power. Allende instituted a series of policies to nationalize major industries such as the American-owned telecommunications industry without compensating Chilean and American investors.[97] The Americans feared, realistically or not, that Allende would ally with the USSR, creating a domino effect for communism in South America.[98] With both the profitability of investors under threat and the possibility of Chile falling in line with the Soviets, Washington took measures to undermine the Allende government. The USA vetoed loans to Chile from multinational financial institutions, and American banks cut off short-term credit, leading to hyperinflation due to Chile printing money to meet its foreign obligations.[99] This sparked an uprising from Chile's middle class due to the prospect that they would lose their wealth from the inflation as well as from Allende's perceived association with the Soviet Union.[100] By 1973, the situation had become critical as the CIA, Chile's middle class, and the military started to undermine the authority of regime. These groups finally decided they had enough of Allende's radical reforms replacing him with Augusto Pinochet, a general in the Chilean military, on 11 September 1973.[101]

After Pinochet's overthrow of Allende's Popular Unity government, the new regime hired a group of economists influenced by Milton Friedman known as the "Chicago Boys".[102] In order to eliminate the policies of the Allende's regime, these economists proposed a programme of radical reforms of market deregulation for the Chilean economy. These recommendations included reducing the size of government, lowering tariff barriers to introduce foreign competition, and privatizing public industries and social programs such as pensions and health care.[103] The regime instituted the recommendations on an ad hoc basis, with the first set of liberalizations in 1975, then again from 1978 to 1981.[104] The overall goal of Pinochet's government was to integrate Chile into the global economy, clamp down on inflation by linking the peso to the US dollar, and loosen trade and financial restrictions. Unlike democratic regimes, Pinochet had complete freedom to repress opposition to the regime, committing thousands of human rights abuses against dissenters. The economic policies made some in Chile very wealthy, namely entrepreneurs, industrialists and the middle class, yet it led a substantial increase in inequality as 3–4 million people fell into poverty due to the chronic underfunding of social programs and highly regressive tax system.[105] The dramatic increase in poverty and inequality would become commonplace in countries that adopted neoliberalism in the 1980s: people on the margins of society would bear the brunt of market liberalization as states reduced taxes and cut back or abolished social programs. The wealthy would benefit from a reduced tax burden, cheaper labour power and gain lucrative investment opportunities.

Under the Pinochet regime, neoliberalism began to reshape the Chilean economy. The liberalization of finance led to a massive amount of foreign investment in Chile. The deregulation of the banks coupled with lax government oversight and low reserve requirements led to an explosion of private lending to both business and individuals.[106] This led to a contradiction in the Chilean economy. In 1982, faltering commodity prices along with overleveraging led to a debt crisis in Chile as banks began to fail.[107] Along with the rest of South America, Chile experienced a severe recession as unemployment increased to nearly 30% while nearly 50% of the population fell below the poverty line.[108] The widespread deregulation of the financial industry almost led to the collapse of the Chilean economy. Despite the rhetoric of free market capitalism,

Pinochet's government ended up nationalizing nearly 70% of the banks, and floated the peso leading to a 60% drop in its value.[109] The private losses due to the deregulation of the financial industry were be subsidized by the state, adding to public debt. From this time onwards, banking regulation was liberalized to attract foreign and domestic investment to provide risky loans with the knowledge the state would step into prevent bank failures. This, in effect, socialized the risk from the financial industry and became commonplace in the 1980s under the presidency of Ronald Reagan.

NOTES

1. Margaret Macmillan. *Paris 1919: Six Months that Changed the World*. (New York: Random House, 2002): 10.
2. The initial payments were set at 132 billion marks or $33 billion for the Germans, but this sum was later cut in half. Moreover, the terms were later changed so the German government could make payments only if it could handle the burden. MacMillan, 480.
3. Barry Eichengreen. *Golden fetters: the gold standard and the Great Depression 1919–1939* (New York: Oxford University Press, 1992): 85.
4. Harold James, *International monetary cooperation since Bretton Woods*, (Washington, D.C. IMF, 1996): 1.
5. The Wall Street Journal. "Dow Jones Industrial Average All-Time Largest One Day Gains and Losses". *Historical Data Index*. Accessed 12 November 2011. Available. http://online.wsj.com/mdc/public/page/2_3047-djia_alltime.html.
6. Ibid.
7. Douglas W. Diamond and Philip H. Dybvig. "Bank Runs, Deposit Insurance, and Liquidity". *Journal of Political Economy*, Vol. 91, No. 3 (Jun., 1983): 401.
8. Ibid.
9. Robert E. Lucas, Jr. and Leonard A. Rapping. "Unemployment in the Great Depression: Is There a Full Explanation?" *Journal of Political Economy*, Vol. 80, No. 1 (Jan.–Feb., 1972): 189.
10. Michael Bernstein, *The Great Depression: Delayed Recovery and Economic Change in America 1929–1939* (Cambridge, Cambridge University Press, 1987): 8.
11. Milton Friedman and Anna Schwartz, *The Great Contraction*. (Princeton, N.J., Princeton University Press, 1965): 25.
12. Bernstein, 13.
13. Ibid., 10.

14. The Economist. "The battle of Smoot-Hawley". 18 December 2008. http://www.economist.com/node/12798595.
15. Eichengreen, 9.
16. Ibid., 18.
17. Ibid., 19.
18. Lisa Keister and Stephanie Moller. "Wealth Inequality in the USA". *Annual Review of Sociology*. Vol. 26, No. 63. (2000): 63.
19. Jonas D.M. Fisher and Andreas Hornstein. "The Role of Real Wages, Productivity, and Fiscal Policy in Germany's Great Depression 1928–1937". *Review of Economic Dynamics*, Vol. 5, No 1: (2002): 150.
20. Ibid., 101.
21. Theda Skocpol. "Political response to capitalist crisis". *Politics & Society*, Vol. 10, No. 2 (March 1980): 159.
22. Ibid., 182.
23. Ibid.
24. James R. Barth, R. Dan Brumbaugh Jr. and James A. Wilcox. "Policy Watch: The Repeal of Glass-Steagall and the Advent of Broad Banking". *The Journal of Economic Perspectives*, Vol. 14, No. 2 (Spring 2000): 194.
25. Ibid., 191.
26. Ibid., 193.
27. Adam Gordon. "The Creation of Homeownership: How New Deal Changes in Banking Regulation Simultaneously Made Homeownership Accessible to Whites and out of Reach for Blacks". *The Yale Law Journal*, Vol. 115, No. 1 (Oct., 2005): 188.
28. Skocpol., 183.
29. James E. Sargent, "The Plot to Seize the White House". *The History Teacher*, Vol. 8, No. 1 (Nov., 1974).
30. Ira Katznelson, Kim Geiger and Daniel Kryder. "Limiting Liberalism: The Southern Veto in Congress, 1933–1950", *Political Science Quarterly* (Vol. 108, No. 2 Summer, 1993), pp. 283–306: 283.
31. Eichengreen, 347.
32. Arthur Meier Schlesinger, *The Coming of the New Deal, 1933–1935* (Boston: Houghton Mifflin, 1957): 9.
33. Ibid., 475.
34. John Maynard Keynes, *The General Theory of Employment, Interest and Money*, (London: Macmillan, 1936).
35. Eichengreen, 205.
36. US Bureau of the Census, *Historical Statistics of the USA, Colonial Times to 1957*. US Government Printing Office (Washington, D.C., 1960): 70.
37. Ibid.
38. Charles Kindleberger, *The World In Depression 1929–1939* (Berkeley, CA, University of California Press, 1986): 11.

39. Ibid., 198.
40. Ibid., 205.
41. M.C. Howard and J.E. King. *The Rise of Neoliberalism in Advanced Capitalism Economies* (New York: Palgrave-Macmillan, 2008).
42. Donald Markwell *John Maynard Keynes and International Relations: Economic Paths to War and Peace* (New York: Oxford University Press: 2006): 210.
43. Quoted in Niall Ferguson, *The Ascent of Money* (New York: Penguin Press, 2008): 306.
44. Williamson Murray and Allan R. Millett. *Military Innovation in the Interwar Period* (Cambridge University Press: New York, 1996): 1.
45. Ibid., 2.
46. Giovanni Arrighi, *The Long Twentieth Century. Money, Power, and the Origins of our Times* (London; New York: Verso, 1994, 2010): 275.
47. C. Randall Henning, *Currencies and Politics in the USA, Germany and Japan* (Washington, DC: Institute for International Economics, 1994): 4
48. Ibid., 44.
49. Peter Alexis Gourevitch. *Politics in Hard Times: Comparative Responses to International Economic Crises* (Ithaca: Cornell University Press, 1986): 18.
50. Ibid.
51. John Lewis Gaddis. *The Cold War: A New History* (New York: Penguin Press 2005): 28–29.
52. John Lewis Gaddis. *Strategies of Containment* (New York; Oxford: Oxford University Press, 2005).
53. For more information see: Tony Smith. "Decolonization and the Response of Colonial Elites". *Comparative Studies in Society and History*. Vol. 20, No. 1. (1978): 20.
54. William Robinson, *Promoting Polyarchy: Globalization, US intervention, and Hegemony* (Cambridge, Cambridge University Press: 1996): 9.
55. William Stueck. *The Korean War: An International History* (Princeton, N.J.: Princeton University Press, 1995): 29.
56. Ibid.
57. Ibid., 36.
58. O. Yul Kwon. "Korean Economic Developments and Prospects" *Asian-Pacific Economic Literature*, Vol. 11, No. 12. (1997): 15.
59. Ibid., 16.
60. Richard Stubbs. "War and Economic Development: Export-Oriented Industrialization in East and Southeast Asia" *Comparative Politics* Vol. 31, No. 3 (Apr., 1999): 345.
61. Kwon, 25.

62. Leland Johnson. "U.S. Business Interests in Cuba and the Rise of Castro". *World Politics.* Vol. 17, No. 3 (Apr., 1965). 443.
63. Matias Travieso-Diazs and Charles P. Trumbull IV, "Foreign Investment in Cuba: Prospects and Perils". *George Washington International Law Review.* Vol. 35, no. 4 (2003): 906.
64. Prabhu L. Pingali and Vo-Tong Xuan. "Vietnam: Decollectivization and Rice Productivity Growth". *Economic Development and Cultural Change.* Vol. 40, No. 4 (Jul., 1992), 697.
65. Stanley Lieberson. "An Empirical Study of Military-Industrial Linkages". *American Journal of Sociology,* Vol. 76, No. 4 (Jan., 1971): 568.
66. Ibid., 569.
67. Stephen Daggett. *CRS Report to Congress: Costs of Major U.S. Wars.* Foreign press centre, US Department of State (24 July 2008). http://fpc.state.gov/documents/organization/108054.pdf. 2.
68. Anthony S. Campagna. *The Economic Consequences of the Vietnam War.* (New York: Praeger, 1991): 38.
69. Ibid., 39.
70. Leo Panitch and Sam Gindin, 14.
71. M.C. Howard and J.E. King, 11.
72. Michael Bordo, Barry Eichengreen and Jongwoo Kim "Was There Really an Earlier Period of International Financial Integration Comparable to Today?" *National Bureau of Economic Research.* Cambridge, MA Working Paper 6738 (1998): 2.
73. Ibid., 3.
74. Eric Helleiner, "Explaining the globalization of financial markets: Bringing states back in". *Review of International Political Economy.* Vol. 2, No. 2, (1995): 322.
75. Campagna, 39.
76. Arrighi, *Adam Smith,* 308.
77. Ibid.
78. Eric Helleiner, *States and the reemergence of global finance: from Bretton Woods to the 1990s* (Ithaca, NY: Cornell University Press, 1994): 13.
79. Ibid., 12.
80. Ibid., 13–14.
81. Ibid., 112.
82. Ibid., 113.
83. The Economist. "A Short History of Modern Finance". *The Economist.* October 16th, 2008. http://www.economist.com/node/12415730.
84. Perry Mehring. *Fischer Black and the Revolutionary Idea of Finance* (Hoboken, N.J.: John Wiley and Sons. 2005): 167.
85. Ibid.

86. Robert Barsky and Lutz Kilian. "Oil and the Macroeconomy Since the 1970s", *National Bureau of Economic Research*, Working Paper No. 10855 (October 2004): 22.
87. Ibid., 15.
88. J. Bradford De Long. "America's Peacetime Inflation: The 1970s", in Christina Romer and David Romer. eds., *Reducing Inflation: Motivation and Strategy* (Chicago: University of Chicago Press, 1997): 269 (247–280).
89. Ibid.
90. Ibid., 270.
91. David Harvey, *The New Imperialism*, 63.
92. David Harvey, *The New Imperialism*, 61.
93. Michael Wallace, "Aggressive Economism, Defensive Control: Contours of American Labour Militancy, 1947–81" *Economic and Industrial Democracy*. Vol. 10, No. 1 (February 1989): 18.
94. Ibid., 30.
95. Howard and King, 208.
96. David Harvey, *A Brief History*, 24.
97. Richard Fagan, "The United States and Chile: Roots and Branches" *Foreign Affairs*, Vol. 53, No. 2 (Jan., 1975): 308.
98. Ibid.,
99. Peter A. Goldberg. "The Politics of the Allende Overthrow in Chile". *Political Science Quarterly*. Vol. 90, No. 1 (Spring, 1975): 108–109.
100. Ibid., 107.
101. Ibid., 113.
102. Angelo Codevilla "Is Pinochet the Model?" *Foreign Affairs*. Vol. 72, No. 5 (November–December, 1993): 134.
103. Ibid.
104. Ibid., 137.
105. Leslie Bethell, *The Cambridge History of Latin America* (Cambridge, Cambridge University Press, 1995): 381.
106. Raphael Bergoeing, Patrick J. Kehoe, Timothy J. Kehoe and Raimundo Soto. "Decade Lost and Found: Mexico and Chile in the 1980s". *National Bureau of Economic Research* Working Paper 8520 (2001): http://www.nber.org/papers/w8520: 11.
107. Ibid.
108. Ibid, 4.
109. Edgardo Barandiarán and Leonardo Hernández, "Origins and Resolution of a Banking Crisis in Chile: 1982–86". *Central Bank of Chile* Working Papers 57 (December 1999): 16.

CHAPTER 3

The Neoliberal Orthodoxy 1979–2000

Economics Are the Method; the Object Is to Change the Heart and Soul.
—Prime Minister Margaret Thatcher.[1]

This chapter will examine the political instiutionalization and normalization of neoliberalism, but recognizes that neoliberalism is not a singular global process. It interrelates with a country's politics, culture and institutions. As was discussed in the last chapter, rather than neoliberalism suddenly becoming mainstream in the 1980s, it began due to the economic and political contradictions of the late 1960s and early 1970s. Even after the election of Margaret Thatcher in 1979 and Ronald Reagan in 1980, the shift towards neoliberalism—the retrenchment of the welfare state, the deregulation of the financial system and the popularization of the "magic of the market"—did not occur immediately, but was part of a longer economic, political and ideational process. Moreover, when traditional centre-left parties returned to power in the 1990s, with Bill Clinton in the USA and Tony Blair in the UK, neoliberal policies were not abandoned in favour of a return to state intervention, but rather championed by so-called progressives.

For the USA and Britain, 1979 proved to be a pivotal year for the popularization of the neoliberal project. In America, the Carter administration appointed Paul Volcker as Federal Reserve chairman with the promise that he would finally get inflation under control. Since the

New Deal the objective of both monetary and fiscal policy had been to achieve full employment, Volcker abandoned this goal and instead focused on lowering inflation regardless of the consequences it might have on employment.[2] Volcker raised interest rates to nearly 20%, a monetary contraction that started a prolonged recession in the USA. In addition, it drove many countries with a high level of debt (such as Chile) into the brink of bankruptcy.[3] In the USA, Britain, Canada and Australia unemployment rates reached over 10% by 1983 due to the sudden contraction of the money supply.[4] The use of monetary policy to quell inflation would be the primary goal of the Federal Reserve from Volcker's tenure onwards. The recession that followed the spike in interest rates, along with failures in foreign policy, contributed to Jimmy Carter's defeat by Ronald Reagan in the 1980 election. The rise of neoliberalism in the USA is often attributed to the policies of the Reagan administration—and indeed he did further deregulate the financial sector—but the deregulation of the financial sector was already well under way by the time he took office.

The Reagan administration instituted polices to undermine any threat to profitability of the wealthy and the financial sector. One of the first policies under his presidency was to substantially lower taxes on top income earners, from 73% to 50%, and cut capital gains taxes to reward investment.[5] Reagan held the belief that by cutting taxes across the board it would facilitate economic growth and therefore government revenue. Though many of Reagan's cuts were scaled back in subsequent pieces of legislation, the overall tax rates for the wealthy continued to drop throughout his time in office.[6] This was part of an overall goal to limit government intervention in the economy, without angering the Republican electoral base. Regardless of the rhetoric of Reagan, politics still matter. Popular government programs such as social security remained untouched, while programs that mainly targeted labour and blacks—a bastion of support for the Democrats—were reduced in scope.[7] More importantly, Reagan altered the popular discourse in the USA on taxes and entrepreneurship:

> Reagan's policy discourse is evidence of the religious zeal with which he condemns the evils of "big government" and proclaims his faith in the inherent goodness of the market. Reagan believes "big government" is a destructive force that restricts competition and opportunity, constrains progress and prosperity, and ultimately erodes the public's work ethic.[8]

While America had a long legacy of scepticism towards government, Reagan's near veneration of the free market changed the popular perspective on the role of government in society. Already, the legacy of conservative domination of Congress meant the USA did not have as comprehensive a welfare state as many European countries.[9] After Reagan, low taxes became a mantra of the Republican Party, and the chanting became much louder after the 2010 midterm elections in which Tea Party candidates were elected to Congress. It became the goal of the Republicans to limit the financial ability of governments to expand the welfare state.

The Reagan administration continued to liberalize the financial sector by further deregulating the savings and loan industry. Yet again, this process started long before Reagan came to office. Under Carter transportation industries including rail, the trucking industry and air travel were all deregulated.[10] At the time there was a Democratic majority in both the House of Representatives and the Senate, so deregulation influenced policy regardless of the political party. By the 1980s, the savings and loan industry, or "thrifts" were deregulated entirely. The industry lent to people to buy a home, finance a car or start a business. The New Deal had set restrictions on the amount of interest on deposits since if a company went bankrupt, the public insurer would have to pay. The Carter administration started the liberalize interest rates, but required companies match this with more insurance.[11] The Reagan administration did away with this insurance and permitted the industry to increase the amount of long-term commercial loans to pay higher interest on deposits.[12] It also allowed lenders to provide 100% financing, eliminating any requirement for a down payment.[13] The Reagan administration believed the market could regulate itself: the savings and loan industry would not provide loans to those at high risk of default, while borrowers would not overburden themselves with an unsustainable level of debt.

As was the case in Chile, the savings and loan industry experienced an economic boom for several years, but this was followed by an unprecedented number of bankruptcies. Initially, investors were attracted to the interest rate premiums compared to regular savings accounts.[14] Large investment firms, such as Merrill Lynch, played a role by connecting investors with this, at the time, lucrative opportunity.[15] Competition within the industry led to an incentive to provide higher interest rates for investors; in order to do so, thrifts took on riskier loans, especially in mortgages.[16] The American housing market increased in value due to the rise in demand created through easy loans. However, by 1986 the housing market started to slow and the failure rate for thrifts started to skyrocket, with over $113 billion worth of losses.[17] By the end of the year, the Federal Savings and Loan Insurance Corporation (FSLIC), the public insurer of the thrift industry, was insolvent.[18] Congress eventually had to intervene to bailout the FSLIC in order to protect the deposits at a cost of over $125 billion to the taxpayer.[19] The collapse of thrifts along with the loss of investor wealth and the value of mortgages played a significant part in leading to the recession in the early 1990s, adding to unemployment and government budget deficits. The failure of the savings and loan industry also started the precedent of bailouts by the federal government to prevent a bank failure from spreading to the overall economy. Similar to Chile, the profits from risky financial ventures were privatized, while the public through the government absorbed the costs in a time of crisis.

Due to the reintroduction of neoliberalism that started in the 1970s, the economies of the USA and Britain had to be transformed to benefit investors and corporations. In order to do so, the post-war consensus between capital and labour had to be broken. In the USA, this started with the air traffic controllers who went on strike in the summer of 1981.[20] The newly inaugurated Reagan administration seized this opportunity to send a clear message to labour: dissent from unions would be met with a harsh response.[21] When the union refused the government's demand to return to work, Reagan decided to fire the striking air traffic controllers and made it illegal for another company to hire a striking worker.[22] These layoffs led to the near collapse of the industry, with many non-certified controllers taking the place of the well-trained workers.[23] Yet this measure sent a message to the workforce and to public sector unions to not interfere with the government's agenda. The Reagan administration would clamp down on labour and ensure profitability for capital. Prior to the 1980s the USA had some strong unions, but the labour movement was not as great of a political force as in some areas of Europe, such as Britain or Germany. However, even with America's history, Reagan represented a different kind of response to union dissent. Though the air traffic controllers were relatively small compared to some of the larger unions, the government would go to extremes to undermine even minor threats to the wealthy.

This was replicated in Britain. Thatcher followed similar tactic to respond to the Coal Miners' Strike of 1984–1985. By the 1980s, foreign competition had greatly undercut the profitability of coal production in the UK. The Thatcher government decided to close down nearly half of the working mines which would lay off nearly 70,000 people over the next 5 years.[24] To do so, the Conservatives had to fight against the National Union of Mineworkers (NUM) one of the country's most powerful and well-organized unions.[25] Unlike the USA, where the air traffic controllers were relatively weak, the coal miners were extremely well organized and had ties to Britain's Labour Party. The strike lasted well over a year and at times became violent as miners clashed with the police.[26] Thatcher's government did not have the financial constraints of the miners. The government could afford to wait out a protracted strike whereas the working-class miners needed their wages to maintain their livelihood and feed their families. So despite taking on one of the most powerful unions in country, the Conservative government won the labour dispute in 1985.[27] The collapse of the union allowed Thatcher to close down half the mines, throwing thousands of people out of work. By the early 1990s, without a strong union to counterbalance the whims of the government, the entire industry was completely privatized.[28] Although Britain had a legacy of worker rights, it could not stop the policies of the Thatcher government, nor the demands of the global financial system.

While the Reagan and Thatcher governments did limit the power of labour, they were only the political apparatus of the newly empowered financial industry. Initially in the 1970s, the liberalization of finance was intended to enhance American policy autonomy and to prolong its hegemonic position in the system. But once deregulated, the financial system placed pressure on these leaders to introduce market-oriented policies and to alter the role of government in the economy. The end of the Bretton Woods system of capital controls forced countries to compete against each other for scarce investment dollars, starting a period of competitive deregulation of labour and financial markets. From this point on, the financial centres of New York and London would vie for foreign investment, resources and talent.[29] The USA started this trend with many other developed countries following suit in the 1980s, such as Germany, France and Japan.[30] Some did so to remain competitive with the USA and the UK, others, like France during the presidency of Francois Mitterrand did so in order to prevent capital flight.[31] And although the process was uneven and varied—some countries, particularly in Scandinavian and Central Europe kept generous welfare states— barriers to finance and foreign investment were progressively lowered in the 1970s and 1980s.[32] Thus, through the hegemonic capabilities of the USA, the ability of global finance to condition and, at times, harm an economy, compelled governments, regardless of their political affiliation, to adopt policies favourable to international investors.

Through the USA, financial markets reshaped the economic policies of a wide variety of governments in the global south through the IMF. Due to the energy crisis of the 1970s and the sudden deregulation of finance, many petroleum exporting countries had excess liquidity and lent out vast sums of money to Brazil, Chile, Argentina and Mexico.[33] By the early 1980s, the spike in interest rates in the USA reduced demand for a wide array of commodities from Latin America ranging from oil to copper. These countries were faced with two problems: higher interest rates made refinancing difficult due to relatively large sums that were borrowed in the 1970s, and they experienced a severe recession compounding their debt.[34] With the prospect of numerous defaults on sovereign debt, the IMF was called upon as a "lender of last resort".[35] However, by the 1980s, the IMF placed new conditions on the terms of the loans. It required countries that received loans undergo a "structural adjustment program" in order to lower state intervention in the economy, devalue the currency, reduce budget deficits and make the economy favourable for international investors.[36] As a result of the IMF conditions, many state enterprises were privatized, wages were repressed and poverty increased among some of the poorest people in Latin America.[37] The IMF—an organization largely financed and its policies are set by the USA—took advantage of an opportunity to make the conditions favourable to finance capital. The USA had already started to deregulate its own economy, and it used its position in the IMF to further weaken state intervention in the global South. From the 1980s onwards, the demands of financiers and investors would take priority over full employment and the regulation of economies in both the developed and developing world.

The 1980s led to neoliberalism as a way to deal with the economic problems of the 1970s. The post-war consensus had been built upon three foundations: a system of regulated currencies, American primacy and a consensus between labour and capital. By the 1980s, contradictions within the capitalist system began to unravel this consensus. In the USA and Britain, interest rates were raised to lower inflation and striking unions were broken. In the USA, which never had a strong welfare state, pro-market policies were more readily adopted. Also the rise in interest rates led to a debt crisis in many countries throughout South America, providing the American-backed IMF the ability to enforce painful structural adjustment programs to attract investment. The international economic system would be reorganized to protect capital and investors. The spatial fixes would no longer be kept within a country, now capital would be able to invest almost anywhere in the world. Countries could be punished by the rapid movement of financial markets.

THERE IS NO ALTERNATIVE? NEOLIBERALISM GOES GLOBAL

By the end of the 1980s, the neoliberal process of accumulation of breaking down barriers and opening previously untapped markets became the new orthodoxy. Neoliberal economic policies coupled with advances in technology allowed finance to move rapidly across borders in search of profit. The dominant western power, the USA, used its centrality in the economic system to compel other countries to liberalize their financial systems. It had a role in international institutions such as the IMF to force countries to adopt market-oriented policies. However, financialization was not an even process; many countries still retained significant control over their domestic economic policies. Nevertheless, by the 1990s pressure from the international financial system or international institutions began to compel countries to adopt market-oriented economic policies. As Panitch and Gindin argue, for the most part, the American economy was strengthened rather than weakened by the financialization of the global economy in the 1980s.[38] America had the unique ability to attract foreign investment capital from foreign markets, and despite ending transferability to gold, the US dollar served as the world's reserve currency. By the late 1980s and early 1990s, these processes appeared to be seamless and beneficial to America: the geopolitical interests of the USA coincided with the accumulation strategies of both domestic capital and international finance. This was also a period of dramatic transformations in the international system. The collapse of competitors to the USA, namely the fall of the Soviet Union and the opening up of China, only further popularized the idea that there was no alternative to neoliberalism.

The end of the Cold War can be partially attributed to the long-term stagnation of the Soviet economy. When Reagan came to power in 1981, his administration took a much more aggressive approach to the Soviet Union with a large military build-up.[39] By 1985, the leader of Soviet Union, Mikhail Gorbachev, recognized the Soviet economy was stagnant—corruption was endemic, and productivity was extremely low—making it difficult for the USSR to compete with the USA.[40] In response to these international and domestic problems, Gorbachev initiated a new period of détente with the USA to reduce military spending, while at the same time instituting glasnost and perestroika to liberalize the Soviet economy. Once these reforms were instituted, the entire Soviet system started to fall apart. By 1989, the Soviet bloc faced a series of revolutions with Communist governments in Eastern Europe overthrown by mass protests. Rather than use the military to suppress these movements, Gorbachev chose to tolerate dissent against the authority of Moscow. Economic and political liberalization proved to be too much for the regime, and the Soviet Union itself dissolved at the end of 1991, ending 50 years of geopolitical tension between the superpowers. The countries of the former Soviet Union ended state control of the economy and adopted many of the free market reforms prescribed by the USA.

The collapse of the USSR was perhaps one of the most important political events of the late twentieth century and was an example of the three processes of working in tandem. First, the USA had been a competitor of the Soviet Union since the end of the Second World War, facing off in series proxy wars. The collapse of the Soviet Union removed the USSR as a threat to American security interests. The USA was the sole remaining global superpower with unmatched military capacities. The heightened tension between the two superpowers was also beneficial to American corporate interests. In 1979, the Soviet Union invaded Afghanistan, and in response the Carter and Reagan, administrations responded through more military spending. For example, in 1980 the USA spent just under $200 billion on defence, by 1988 defence spending increased to almost $350 billion per year (all figures in $US 1995).[41] Furthermore, Washington proposed the Strategic Defense Initiative (SDI) to use lasers to shoot down incoming warheads (a program that as of 2012 has yet to yield any positive results), making the 1980s a very profitable time for defence contractors and other related military industries.[42] The increase in defence spending had the added bonus of promoting job growth, which aided Reagan in his re-election campaign in 1984. The collapse of the Eastern bloc led to the liberalization of the economies in the former USSR, which opened up new markets for American consumer goods.[43]

The changes in the financial system were a determinant in the downfall of communism as well. When the Reagan administration bolstered defence spending, it also reduced taxes on the upper and middle class, leading to nearly quadrupling US public debt to $4 trillion by 1992.[44] Despite the profligacy of the American government, it had the ability to attract capital in order to continue to finance this debt. Moreover, since the dollar was no longer pegged, countries did not have a method to exchange their US dollar reserves for gold. Since US treasuries were considered to be the safest investment, their yields—and the cost of borrowing—remained low, this provided the American government with greater fiscal flexibility to spend without having to raise taxes or cut entrenched and popular social programs.[45] Financialization allowed the USA to borrow enough money to outspend the Soviet Union. Certainly, this was not the only reason the Soviet Union collapsed, but it did give the Americans a financial advantage over its competitor. Furthermore, after the collapse of communism, an unexploited market was now open to investors. Initially, investment started slowly and unevenly as countries transitioned towards market economies in the early to mid-1990s, but by the 2000s there was massive investment from banks in Western Europe, particularly in more market-friendly countries such as the Czech Republic, Hungary and Slovenia.[46] Many of these countries privatized their telecommunications industry and public utilities which were subsequently purchased by investors from Western Europe.[47] Some Eastern European countries joined the European Union to facilitate greater trade and attract investment. So the liberalization of finance gave the Americans the ability to outspend the Soviet Union, and eventually profited from the opening of new markets to investment.

Also during the 1980s, the economy was opened in the most heavily populated country in the world: China. By the 1970s, the long-standing split between the PRC and the USSR led China to open diplomatic relations with the USA. From a geo-strategic perspective, it was to America's advantage to normalize relations in order to draw China into the western fold away from the Soviet Union.[48] The political opening of China was shortly followed by economic openness after the death of Mao in 1976 and the ascension of Deng Xiaoping.[49] By the 1980s, Deng introduced reforms to China's legal and economic system, slowly opening the country to foreign investment.[50] At the time, China was a poor agricultural society—Mao's Cultural Revolution and Great Leap Forward killed millions and left the economy in ruins. The purpose of these reforms were to gradually introduce capitalism but with state oversight over banks and corporations. Some degree of private ownership was tolerated, but the government still maintained a controlling share.[51] During the 1980s, the experimentation met with success—China could attract low-wage low-skill industries and export goods to the USA.[52] However, this development was not without some problems: China's economic development was hampered by trade sanctions after the government brutally crushed dissenters during the Tiananmen Square protests in 1989. Learning from the successes of the 1980s, the Chinese government fully opened its economy to foreign investment in the 1990s and began to grow at an unprecedented rate, finally joining the WTO in 2001, adopting most global trade and investment standards.[53]

By the late 1990s, the former USSR and China were starting to be integrated into the global capitalist system. As foreign investment regulations were deregulated throughout the world, financial markets gained the ability to enrich or punish a country's economy at an unprecedented speed. Moreover, after a brief recession in the early 1990s, most economies in the developed world entered a prolonged period of economic growth due the technological advancements in computers and information technologies. This tech boom coupled with the opening of China led to a substantial increase in Global Production Networks (GPN) where firms produced goods where labour was cheap and sold them to consumers in the developed world.[54] One such example, the American retailer Wal-Mart became one of the world's largest companies in the 1990s by streamlining the production process. Wal-Mart gathered information at the point of sale to automatically generate production orders in China, cutting down on overall costs.[55] Corporations were increasingly taking advantage of deregulated markets and loose financial restriction in order to produce on a global level. The liberalization of finance was supposedly beneficial to both Chinese workers and American consumers. China had a vast pool of workers and wealthy American consumers could purchase Chinese-made products at a lower price. By the 1990s, policies to retrench government and liberalize finance and production were widely instituted by politicians throughout developed and developing economies.

In the 1990s, many of the conservative parties that enacted neoliberal policies were defeated and traditional centre-left parties were given the opportunity to govern. In the USA, the Democrat Bill Clinton was elected president in 1992 and in Britain Tony Blair's Labour Party attained a majority in parliament in 1997. Once in power, though, Clinton and Blair continued many of the same policies as their predecessors. Clinton cut government spending, lowered taxes on corporations and the wealthy and reformed welfare. In the UK, Blair broke with the old affiliations to the labour movement and promised a "third way" between the free market agenda of the Conservatives and socialism.[56] There are many reasons for this continuity, but paramount was the ability of financial markets to force governments to comply with demands of international investors. By 1995, according to the Bank of International Settlements (BIS) over $1.2 trillion dollars were traded over currency exchanges per day in investments, swaps and derivatives.[57] By the 1990s, many developed and developing countries, with the exception of India and China where the government still played a large role, had removed capital controls completely.[58] The massive amount of investment dollars move with little regulatory oversight across international boundaries. The sheer size and volume of global financial markets made any government, regardless of its size in the global economy, cater to the demands of international investors in order to prevent volatility in financial markets.

The liberalization of finance was not without a tendency towards crisis. In the 1990s, a series of sudden and rapid panics occurred in emerging economies. The first significant panic was in Mexico after the government deregulated capital controls. Mexico was neither heavily in debt by global standards nor did it have an overly expansive welfare state, yet investors lost confidence and the value of the peso collapsed.[59] Since borrowing costs had risen due to the rapid devaluation of the peso, the Americans provided Mexico with a bailout to prevent a default on their debt and the crisis from spreading. A similar panic occurred in 1997 in East Asia, a region that had developed quickly since the 1970s. When Thailand floated its currency, investors set off a speculative run against the economy. The crisis quickly spread to South Korea, Malaysia, the Philippines and Indonesia threatening the region's banks and stock markets.[60] In order to mitigate the crisis, the IMF provided these countries with US $95 billion in loans to restore the confidence of international investors and calm financial markets.[61] However, the IMF required a series of difficult austerity measures as part of the loan conditions—the countries had to cut government spending and increase taxes.[62] The Asian financial crisis had one other significant ramification: it weakened the already fragile Russian economy. Similar to the Asian crisis, the IMF offered the government of Russia a loan package. Yet financial markets proved too powerful for the IMF and undermined the value of the Ruble, leading a default on the country's debt in 1998.[63] Though Russia started to recover by 1999, the political damage had been done: Russia fell back into authoritarianism under the presidency of Vladimir Putin.

By the year 2000, in advanced economies, capital markets had been deregulated allowing investors to move money quickly and with minimal government oversight. Even corporations that produced goods would often use their assets to leverage in order to lower costs through global production chains. Deregulation would often lead to an asset bubble as investors rush in for quick profit, followed by a crisis that undermined the economic stability of a country. The US government, either directly or through an intermediary like the IMF, would act as lender of last resort or intervene to prevent the panic from spreading. A discussed earlier, the East Asian and Russian crisis continued a pattern of targeted bailouts to prevent a systemic crisis. For developing countries, loans came with the conditions to retrench government spending and to cater to the interests of international investors. At the end of Clinton's term in office, America had unquestionably benefited from the liberalization of capital markets. The advances in technology led to a high level of employment, while trade with China kept inflation low and provided the country with cheap imports. Though there had been periodic crises throughout the 1990s in emerging economies, for the most part, the problems had been contained. With the USA acting in the interests of international investors, it seemed that there was no alternative to neoliberalism.

By the turn of the millennium, it appeared the American government, corporations and international investors worked together to spread capitalism. With China and Russia being brought into the global economy, there was no longer any viable alternative to capitalism. Even India started to open its economy in the 1990s to foreign investment. However, underlying the supposed unity of the American government, corporations, developed and emerging economies and finance there were marked differences and new sources of conflict. Systemic fault lines appeared between those that benefited from this phase of free market capitalism and those that did not. For developed economies, Canada, the USA and Mexico signed the North American Free Trade Agreement in the early 1990s, while a single currency, the Euro, started to become adopted by continental European countries in the year 1999. It was during the late 1990s that the antiglobalization movement gained support. People protested against the neoliberal agenda of the G8 and WTO arguing that it exacerbated global inequality and led to the exploitation of the developing world as countries "raced to the bottom" for investment.[64] Corporate practices were scrutinized by activists who argued many workers in developing economies were poorly paid and had few employment rights.[65] Many journalists and academics argued the new economic order gave too much power to corporations, banks and financial markets at the expense of democracy and human rights.[66] It is no coincidence that Hardt and Negri's assumption that economic and political power had become harmonized was a product of the experience of the 1990s.[67] In their view, *Empire* represented the synchronization of an economic, political and cultural process that exploited the global multitude.

With the demise of the Soviet Union and the opening of China, there were no longer any remaining major geopolitical threats to America. Washington was free to use its role as the sole superpower to promote American corporate interests and integrate previously untapped markets into the world economy. Corporations could use China and Eastern Europe as cheap sources of labour, lowering the price of goods to sell to wealthier countries. The quick movement of finance compelled governments to deregulate their financial sector in order to attract investment. Although this led to the need to bailout Mexico and East Asian countries, for the most part, the 1990s were a profitable time for investors. The dot-com boom in the USA led to one of the longest periods of economic growth in the USA since the 1960s. In the 2000 presidential election between the Democrat Al Gore and the Republican George W. Bush, the debate centred upon how the federal government should spend its projected surpluses. However, this peace and prosperity proved to be short-lived as the events of the next decade, as well as the decisions made by George W. Bush as president, produced tensions and contradictions between the financial system and American government.

THE BUSH WARS

The Bush administration's poorly executed invasion of Iraq as a response to the terrorist attacks of September 11th, 2001 began tension in the seemingly harmonious process between the spread of capitalist markets and the objectives of American foreign policy. The purpose of this section will be to examine the broader systemic processes that took place in the post-9/11 period. Similar to previous Cold War conflicts, there was no dominant economic motive for the invasion of Iraq for the Americans. Though there are vast oil reserves in Iraq, the war, if anything, has not proved beneficial to the American economy nor American corporations. The war in Iraq was in fact a new phase of American dominance, one led by neoconservatives. The Bush administration promised to spread democracy, freedom and markets in the Middle East as a method to ensure the security of Americans. The domestic circumstances in a post-9/11 context were a major determinant behind the invasion. Although the war in Iraq was costly for the American government, for many firms, it has been extremely profitable. Investors in military and oil corporations, particularly those from China and Russia, profited from the war at the expense of the American government.

As a response to the terrorist attacks of 11 September 2001, the USA started a series of military invasions in order to bring greater domestic security. For the American government, "The War on Terror" became a priority rather than just economic liberalization. Although the USA's commitment to free trade and open markets was not abandoned completely, the war on terror became a paramount consideration for the Bush administration.[68] As a consequence of the attacks, NATO launched the war in Afghanistan hoping to eliminate Al-Qaeda and the Taliban. The war was viewed by most as a multilateral conflict that had the support, or at least the tacit acceptance, of the international community. The Bush administration went through institutional channels for the war and attained the consent of the UN to launch an attack on Afghanistan. For the war on terror, geopolitical interests took priority. The USA had been attacked by a sub-state terrorist organization, and, at least for this conflict, was willing to work through the UN to attain a sense of international legitimacy for the war. However, this conciliatory approach was shortly thereafter rejected as the USA launched a war that violated of international law and infuriated its allies.

In the spring of 2003, the Bush administration decided to invade Iraq with a coalition of willing countries, but without the consent of the UN. There were many reasons given by the Americans for the removal of Saddam Hussein by force. The administration argued that Saddam was a security threat to the USA and likely would harbour terrorists and provide them with weapons of mass destruction.[69] However, this justification was widely refuted by the American security establishment. As John Mearsheimer and Steven Walt argue, even with nuclear weapons, Iraq could easily be contained and posed little threat to international peace.[70] During the 1991 Gulf War when Iraq invaded Kuwait, the Americans led a coalition to remove Iraq's forces. Saddam was left in power in Iraq, but the regime was essentially isolated from the international community, posing a negligible threat to the region.[71] Yet despite these protests from the security establishment, the threat of WMDs was cited as a major reason to use force to oust Saddam.

Another justification for the invasion was to spread democracy to Iraq.[72] American liberal scholars and policy-makers have an ideological commitment to democracy. And although in practice the USA government has supported right-wing dictators throughout Latin America and Southeast Asia, by 2001 many Republicans believed that the best method to ensure America's security and economic prosperity was through regime change in the Middle East.[73] Bush stated in a weekly radio address in 2005: "A democratic Iraq will be a powerful setback to the terrorists who seek to harm our nation... A democratic Iraq will be a great triumph in the history of liberty. And a democratic Iraq will be a source of peace for our children and grandchildren".[74] The war in Iraq was an attempt by the Bush administration to bring democracy to a region through the use of force. Bush's decision was at least in part a way to combat hostile regimes. There was a belief that a democratic Iraq would not pose a threat to American interests and would not be a launching ground for terrorist cells. Of course, the war did not go as planned and democratic institutions in Iraq remain fragile. But at least on the part of the Americans, regime change was a determinant behind the decision to invade.

Though the USA lost international prestige and economic resources, the protracted conflict in Iraq has been beneficial to the financial industry and TNCs. As with Vietnam, the war has been profitable for specific industries. The Americans provided contracts to develop Iraq's oil to companies such as Halliburton and British Petroleum until 2007 when Indian, Chinese and Russian companies took over.[75] Certainly these corporations profited from the war and Halliburton had ties to the Bush administration, but as the war went on, other firms were awarded Iraq's oil contracts. Also since these corporations are, for the most part, publicly traded companies, regardless of where the oil is sold, the profits go back to the shareholders of these corporations, whether it be international investors or, in the case of Chinese firms, the Chinese Communist Party. The reconstruction and security costs, upwards of $50 billion a year, were paid by the American government with over a third going to private security firms.[76] Common in the neoliberal process, throughout the war the costs have been paid by American taxpayers, and a government that has grown its debt to fight this war, while the profits have been privatized.[77] The group that has profited from the war in Iraq has been investors. Geopolitical interests may have been a major determinant of the American invasion, but the opportunity soon arose for corporations and investors to profit from the war at the expense of the Americans. Capital, though it was not the only driving force behind the initial invasion, took advantage of the situation once the Americans overthrew Saddam's regime. So though capitalism was a factor, the ideological commitment of Bush administration to democracy and the perceived national security threats were large determinants of the invasion.

Whether the Iraq war was motivated by the by the Bush administration's desire to prolong American hegemony, or whether it proves to be a harbinger of the end of USA remains uncertain. By all measures—in terms of lives and money spent—the war was expensive for the Americans and, as of yet, has shown very little direct return for the US government. Some American firms have profited from the initial few years of the conflict, but, in the end, it was international investors that have gained the most. As Arrighi suggests the war was an economic drain for the Americans—taxes were cut by the Bush administration and the war was financed by large deficits, often borrowing money from the Chinese.[78] Yet there was no massive financial or geopolitical crisis as a result of America's unilateralism, nor did the invasion of Iraq foreshadow further American interventions into regimes such as North Korea or Iran. And although the USA went further in debt due to the war, financial markets continued to function normally with the ability to borrow cheaply from the savings glut in Southeast Asia. It would take a domestic housing market crisis before the effects of neoliberalism began to challenge the political and economic power of the USA.

Summary

The purpose of this chapter has been to analyse the development of the financial system and American hegemony throughout the twentieth century. I traced the historical rise of the USA after the Second World War, and how it has been trying to manage, albeit with varying degrees of success, the global capitalist system. The material transformation of capitalism was assessed throughout this chapter, from the near collapse of global trade and finance during the depression, to its regulation in the post-war era. It seemed countries had learned from the depression and sought to institute a framework to foster a compromise with labour and capital. In the immediate post-war period, corporations often worked in tandem with the American government—when business interests were threatened, the US military intervened. Yet, there were other motivations for the USA than just promoting business interests. The threat of the spread of communism compelled the USA to expend vast military and economic resources to prevent the spread of communism. These two interrelated processes of American military expansion and the opening of markets for investment defined the post-war system, with America as the dominant hegemon of the capitalist system.

The contradictions in capitalism of the 1970s gave way to the incremental rise of neoliberalism. There were many determinants that led to this transition. One reason was the very way the post-WWII regime was constructed with the USA as the centre of the global economy. The Bretton Woods system had created a stable international economic order that relied upon the Americans to underwrite the system. By the 1970s, the rapid growth in competition from Europe and Japan, along with the power of the labour movement and the toll of the Vietnam War, led to the unravelling of the post-war consensus. This started with an economic decision of the Nixon administration to suspend the US dollar's convertibility to gold, thereby undermining the entire Bretton Woods system of currency controls. This proved to be a short-term solution, but had unforeseen consequences. It paved the way for broader deregulation in the global economy. The energy crises of the 1970s led to a decade of high inflation and low economic growth that further destabilized the post-war consensus. Although the degree to which neoliberalism was adopted was uneven, it set off the new phase—the ability of corporations and finance to condition and penalize a country that goes against market principles.

When the Soviet Union collapsed and China started on its path to reform, capital has fewer barriers in the global economy. By the 1990s, the USA government, international financial institutions and corporations worked in tandem to open markets and protect the rights of investors. Even traditional centre-left parties in the USA and the UK had adopted pro-market policies. And though there were periodic crises in Mexico, South Asia and Russia, the Americans and the IMF were available to prevent a broader systemic crisis of capitalism. By the turn of the millennium, it seemed as though the processes of American expansionism and neoliberal markets had harmonized. Yet despite the seeming synchronization of these forces, by 2001 tensions began to arise between the USA and the financial system. In the post 9/11 period, these interests began to diverge with the American-led invasions of Iraq and Afghanistan, yet it would take the global crisis of the Great Recession to show that fault lines in the American political system.

NOTES

1. Ronald Butt "Interview with Margaret Thatcher". *The Sunday Times*, May 3rd, 1981.
2. Harvey, *A Brief History of Neoliberalism*, 23.
3. Harvey, *A Brief History of Neoliberalism*, 23.
4. Joyanna Moy. "Recent Trends in Unemployment and the Labor Force: 10 Countries". *Monthly Labor Review*, Bureau of Labor Statistics 108: 8 (1985): 9.
5. Office of Tax Analysis *Revenue Effects of Major Tax Bills*. United States Department of the Treasury. Working Paper 81, 2003, rev (September 2006): 12.
6. Harvey, *A Brief History of Neoliberalism*, 26.
7. Paul Pierson, "When Effect Becomes Cause: Policy Feedback and Political Change The Three Worlds of Welfare Capitalism by Gosta Esping-Andersen; The Political Power of Economic Ideas: Keynesianism across Countries by Peter Hall; Institutions, Institutional Change and Economic Performance by Douglass C. North; Protecting Soldiers and Mothers: The Political Origins of Social Policy in the United States by Theda Skocpol" *World Politics*, Vol. 45, No. 4 (Jul., 1993): 595.
8. Michael Weiler and W. Barnett Pearce. *Reagan and Public Discourse in America* (Tuscaloosa: University of Alabama Press, 1992): 261.
9. Gosta Esping-Andersen *The Three Worlds of Welfare Capitalism* (Cambridge England: Polity Press, 1990).
10. Bart M. Lambrecht "The Impact of Debt Financing on Entry and Exit in a Duopoly" *Review of Financial Studies*. Vol. 14, No. 3, (2001): 766.
11. Kitty Calavita and Henry N. Pontell "Savings and Loan Industry "Heads I Win, Tails You Lose": Deregulation, Crime, and Crisis in the Savings and Loan Industry". *Crime & Delinquency*. Vol. 36 (1990): 313.
12. Ibid.
13. Ibid.
14. Lawrence J. White, "A Cautionary Tale of Deregulation Gone Awry: The S&L Debacle" *Southern Economic Journal*. Vol. 59, No. 3 (Jan., 1993): 509.
15. Calavita and Pontell, 92.
16. Timothy Curry and Lynn Shibut "The Cost of the Savings and Loan Crisis: Truth and Consequences" *FDIC Review* Vol. 13 No. 2. Washington, DC. (December 2000): 26.
17. Ibid., 27.
18. Ibid., 30.
19. Ibid., 31.
20. Willis J. Nordlund, *Silent Skies: the Air Traffic Controllers' Strike* (Westport, Connecticut: Praeger Publishing, 1998): 13.

21. Ibid., 14.
22. Ibid., 14.
23. Ibid., 15.
24. Jonathan Winterton and Ruth Winterton, *Coal crisis, and conflict: the 1984–85 miners' strike in Yorkshire* (Manchester; New York: Manchester University Press, 1989): 42.
25. Ibid., 9.
26. Ibid., 9.
27. Ibid., 10.
28. Thomas Clarke, "The Political Economy of the UK privatization Programme" in *The Political Economy of Privatization*. By Thomas Clarke and Christos Pitelis (London; New York: Routledge, 1993): 210.
29. Saskia Sassen "Global Financial Centers" *Foreign Affairs*. Vol. 78, No. 1 (Jan. –Feb., 1999): 75.
30. Ibid., 78.
31. Craig Parsons, *A Certain Idea of Europe* (Ithaca; London: Cornell University Press, 2003): 171.
32. Helleiner. "Explaining the globalization of financial markets", 325.
33. Ilene Grabel "Crossing Boarders a Case for Cooperation in International Financial Markets" *Creating A New World Economy: Forces of Change and Plans for Action*. Eds. Gerald A. Epstein, Julie Graham and Jessica Nembhard (Philadelphia, Pa: Temple University Press, 1993): 70.
34. Ibid.
35. Manuel Pastor, Jr, "Latin America, the Debt Crisis, and the International Monetary Fund" *Latin American Perspectives*, Vol. 16, No. 1, (Winter, 1989): 91.
36. Ibid., 92.
37. Ibid., 94.
38. Leo Panitch and Sam Gindin "Contours and Sources of Imperial Finance" In Leo Panitch and Martijn Konings *American Empire and the Political Economy of Global Finance* (Basingstoke: Palgrave Macmillan, 2009): 32.
39. Fred Chernoff "Ending the Cold War: The Soviet Retreat and the US Military Buildup" *International Affairs*, Vol. 67, No. 1 (Jan., 1991): 124.
40. Ibid.
41. Vidhan K Goyala, Kenneth Lehnb and Stanko Racicb, "Growth Opportunities and Corporate Debt Policy: the Case of the U.S. Defense Industry" *Journal of Financial Economics*. Vol. 64, No. 1, (April 2002): 38.
42. Robert W. DeGrasse Jr. and M.E. Sharpe, "Military Expansion Economic Decline: The Impact of Military Spending on U.S. Economic Performance" *Journal of Policy Analysis and Management*. Vol. 3 (Spring 1984): 482.

43. Stephen Gill, "Economic Globalization and the Internationalization of Authority: Limits and Contradictions", *Geoforum*. Vol. 23 No. 3 (1992): 270.
44. Benjamin M. Friedman "Deficits and Debt in the Short and Long Run" *National Bureau of Economic Research* Working Paper No. 11630 (October 2005): 20.
45. William Bonner and Addison Wiggin, *Empire of Debt* (Wiley: Hoboken, New Jersey; 2006): 202.
46. Pradeep Mitra, Marcelo Selowsky, Juan Zalduendo *Turmoil at Twenty: Recession, Recovery, and Reform in Central and Eastern Europe* (Washington, DC: World Bank, 2010): 6.
47. Saul Estrin, Xavier Richet, Josef C. Brada *Foreign Direct Investment in Central Eastern Europe: Case Studies of Firms in Transition* (Armonk, N.Y.: M.E. Sharpe, 2000): xvii.
48. Warren I. Cohen, *America's Response to China: A History of Sino-American Relations* (New York: Columbia University Press, 2010): 219.
49. Harvey, *A Brief History of Neoliberalism*, 120.
50. Ibid., 124.
51. Ibid., 125.
52. Ibid., 130.
53. Ibid.
54. Dieter Ernst and Linsu Kim, "Global Production Networks, Knowledge Diffusion, and Local Capability Formation" *Research Policy*. Vol. 31. No. 8–9 (December 2002): 1417.
55. Peter Berg, Eileen Appelbaum, Thomas Bailey, Arne Kalleberg "The Performance Effects of Modular Production in the Apparel Industry" *Industrial Relations: A Journal of Economy and Society*. Vol. 35, No. 3 (July 1996): 357.
56. Anthony Giddens, *The Third Way: the Renewal of Social Democracy* (Malden, Mass: Polity Press, 1998): vii.
57. Bank For International Settlements.*Triennial Central Bank Survey of Foreign Exchange and Derivatives Market Activity 1995—Final results* (May 1996): www.bis.org/publ/r_fx98.htm: 3.
58. Joseph Stiglitz *Globaliztion and Its Discontents* (New York: W. W. Norton & Co., 2002): 125.
59. J Sachs, A Tornell and Andrés Velasco "The Mexican peso crisis: Sudden death or death foretold?" *Journal of International Economics*. Vol. 41, No. 3–4, (1996): 268.
60. Stiglitz, 89.
61. Stiglitz, 95.
62. Stiglitz, 96.
63. Stiglitz,150.

64. Noam Chomsky, *Profit Over People: Neoliberalism and the Global Order* (New York: Seven Stories Press, 1999): 13.
65. Naomi Klein *No Logo* (Toronto: Knopf Canada, 2000).
66. Chomsky, 11.
67. Hardt and Negri, *Empire*, 6.
68. Ibid.
69. John Mearsheimer and Stephen Walt "An Unnecessary War" *Foreign Policy*. 134 January/February (2003): 52.
70. Ibid.
71. Ibid.
72. Robert G Kaufman. *In the Defense of the Bush Doctrine* (Lexington: University Press of Kentucky, 2007).
73. David Frum and Richard Perle *An End to Evil* (New York: Random House. 2004).
74. George W. Bush. *Presidential Radio Address*. June 25th 2005. Available: http://www.presidency.ucsb.edu/ws/index.php?pid=58777#axzz1kPZMEnpk
75. PW Singer "Outsourcing War" *Foreign Affairs*. Vol. 84 (August 2005): 123.
76. Michael Bhatia "Postconflict Profit: The Political Economy of Intervention" *Global Governance*. Vol. 11, No. 2 (Apr.–June 2005): 206.
77. Singer, 123.
78. Arrighi, *Adam Smith in Beijing*, 226.

CHAPTER 4

A Crisis in the European Union

The Great Recession has led many scholars to question the hegemony of the USA, which was at the centre of the crisis. Since the 1980s, the American government has promoted the financialization of both the US and global economy. Financing was used to overcome barriers to accumulation, opening up new untapped markets for profit. In the USA, lax credit requirements integrated lower income Americans into the financial system. Meanwhile, the savings of people in China was used to keep interest rates in the USA low, perpetuating a credit bubble by linking American consumers to the Chinese economy. When periodic crises occurred prior 2008, it was usually in emerging economies, such as South America in the 1980s and Southeast Asia in the 1990s. The subprime mortgage crisis of 2008 showed the USA was just as vulnerable to global finance as any other economy. Moreover, America was the hub of a financial system, so the contagion quickly spread to Europe and Asia becoming a truly global financial crisis. After the crisis began, the power of the financial system has continued to be dominant process that conditions the global economy.

The financial crisis cannot be understood without a broader understanding of the global expansion of capitalism in South Asia, the complexity of the financial system, and the specifics of the American housing market. Neoliberalism arose out of the contradictions in the post-war consensus. After the collapse of the Soviet Union and the opening of China, there were fewer international barriers to investment and profit. The reduction of these barriers led to an explosion of global investment capital, particularly in East Asia. However, along with the growth in scope of the financial system, its ability to rapidly undermine the strength of an economy also grew as discussed previously with the 1997 Asian Financial Crisis. Yet, when periodic crises occurred, the American government was available to provide assistance and prevent a broader downturn in the global economy. Prior to 2008, it seemed as though major developed countries benefited from the financialization of markets, with the USA retaining its status of hegemon for nearly two decades after the fall of the USSR. Yet the very method for prolonging America's dominance through the liberalization of finance led to a contradiction in the global economy in 2008, with the USA at the centre.

Since the crisis of 2008, the recession has spread throughout the global economy. Though the crisis is global, linking countries and regions together through the international financial system, each region has experienced it in unique ways based on numerous domestic factors. The purpose of this chapter is to explore the consequences of the recession in each major region in the global economy. Within the global financial system, each country is trying to manage its place within the global capitalist system. For the USA as I will discuss later, with its divided branches of government, the recession has brought about a variety of populist movements against the intervention of the government in the economy. Initially, both the Bush and Obama administrations enacted policies to help manage the effects of the crisis, but since the economic downturn has been protracted, the polarization of American politics has led to political deadlock over the appropriate response of the government to the recession. This almost led to a default on US debt—a historically unprecedented event that would have been an economic catastrophe.

For countries in Europe, the problems are related to the debt levels brought on by the recession and the monetary restrictions of the Euro. The main determinants of the crisis in Europe are political, economic and institutional. Financial markets will not lend the PIIGS money which only further raises borrowing costs. The prospect of a looming default undermines confidence in the Euro. Due to the institutional restrictions of the EU, the policy options are limited: the PIIGS cannot devalue their currencies, nor can they engage in quantitative easing like the American government. Instead, they have become reliant upon wealthier countries like Germany and France for periodic bailouts and been forced to adopt painful austerity measures. If a country is forced to leave, or there are widespread defaults, there is fear that it could lead to another panic and spread to other countries.

The Eurozone Crisis

The period following the financial crisis has, if anything, shown the ability of financial markets to condition the economics and politics of states throughout Europe. The subprime contagion quickly spread, albeit to varying degrees, to the rest of the global economy. Initially, in response to the crisis, there was a great deal of consensus between countries over how to mitigate the impact of the crisis: countries would effectively absorb the costs of their financial institutions, thereby nationalizing private losses. However, by 2010, financial unevenness in the global economy began to re-emerge. In countries tied to the Euro, this mounting debt led a sovereign debt crisis in many regions as international investors dumped bonds from European countries out of fear of a default. The events since the crisis have led to growing conflict between in almost every major economy. In each case, with the exception of China for unique reasons, the demands of domestic politics, regional and location and financial markets have led to the political and economic conflict. For the EU, capital markets have threatened the stability of the Eurozone, forcing governments to adopt painful and unpopular austerity measures.

The ongoing debt crisis has revealed the shortcomings of Europe's monetary union to allow countries to deal with a debt crisis; this will likely cripple the EU for years to come. The strains imposed by the ongoing debt crisis will only be protracted by the inability of the Americans and Europeans to adequately deal with crisis. Yet again, Gowan and Harvey provide valuable theoretical insights into the rising tensions within Europe and between the Eurozone and the USA. During the period immediately following the adoption of the Euro, Europe's loose monetary union seemed to benefit every country that was involved.[1] European firms were able to sell their goods with fewer barriers in Eurozone markets, and European governments were able to take advantage of the lower interest rates that resulted from what was essentially the supranationalization of the Deutschmark. During the 2000s when the global economy was relatively prosperous, the situation worked out well. Germany could sell its goods in an open market with limited trade restrictions and southern Europeans counties could borrow at low rates to fund their social expenditure.

However, the 2008 financial crisis and the subsequent recession have highlighted the problems associated with trying to develop a common currency for a region as varied as the Eurozone. The 17 countries that use the Euro are bound by treaty commitments to abide by the policies set out by the European Central Bank (ECB), which sets interest rates for the Eurozone. Nonetheless, a true fiscal union does not exist between EU member-states. Guidelines do exist to limit overall debt-to-GDP ratios and curtail annual deficit spending, but the enforcement mechanism for these rules is weak and is often disregarded by the more powerful countries in the EU.[2] At the national level, each country sets its own budget, allocates its resources according to its own priorities and accumulates its own sovereign debt. Contrary to the assumptions of Hardt and Negri, this has led to high degree of incoherence in European policy, as well as sparking a crisis between prudent northern European countries and the spendthrift south. In contrast their northern counterparts, Mediterranean governments chose to borrow cheaply using the favourable interest rates that they gained through the adoption of the Euro.

Immediately after the crisis, the Americans were involved as was the IMF to provide financing for the troubled economies in Europe. However, over time Washington has become more inward-looking and reluctant to take a leadership role in problems on the continent. Contrary to the expectations of Panitch and Gindin, the USA has withdrawn politically and economically from the European debt crisis. In a meeting of the G20 in November 2011, Obama pledged the USA would not offer further financial assistance to beleaguered European economies.[3] This is due to America's own debt problems, but it is also motivated by domestic political concerns. The Obama administration has difficulty convincing its Congress to spend money on its own economic issues without the added burden of providing more financing for Europe. This is a clear indication of domestic American politics taking priority over the demands of the financial system since the fallout of a sovereign default would likely harm the entire global economy.[4] As we can see, the tensions arising have begun to create conflict between major capitalist countries. Financial markets are compelling wealthier countries to provide money for southern European countries, but domestic politics prevents more comprehensive policies to deal with the sovereign crisis. It is now up to the Europeans through the ECB and EFSF to prevent the crisis from spreading from Greece to Italy and other indebted countries. The USA no longer is willing, or able, to take an active role as the lender of last resort in times of crisis. The withdrawal of the USA from international financial affairs has left an opening for other regional and international powers to fill the void.

As a result of this borrowing and the crisis, a major sovereign debt crisis has occurred in Portugal, Italy, Ireland, Greece and Spain (PIIGS), all of which, with the exception of Ireland, accumulated high levels of debt in the years prior to 2008. So far, it is the Greek economy that has teetered closest to a full default, reaching an unsustainable 140% debt-to-GDP ratio in 2011.[5] Financial markets, sensing that Greece is unable to carry such a large debt given the size of its economy fled Greek bonds, driving up borrowing costs. In response, Germany, France and the IMF have provided ad hoc bailouts through the European Financial Stability Facility (EFSF) in order to prevent a default that could undermine the Euro and lead to a broader crisis in the Eurozone. But despite receiving billions of Euros in aid, Greek 10-year bond yields remained high, indicating a low degree of investor confidence in Greece's long-term economic prospects.[6] This is partially due to the unpopularity of the austerity measures demanded by Germans in return for bailouts. The situation has deteriorated to the point where German and French leaders have started to openly discuss the possibility of an orderly default, in recognition that Greece is too deeply in debt to ever pay back investors.

The issues surrounding Greece's looming possible default have profound implications for the long-term economic prospects of the Eurozone as a whole. In responding to this crisis, European leaders have been forced to choose between three untenable courses of action, all of which have the potential to undermine the European Union and its common currency. The first option open to European governments is to continue to provide bailouts to its insolvent members on an ad hoc basis; by drawing upon the resources of its richer members and the IMF, the EU's leaders can stave off the immediate threat of default. So far this has been the policy adopted for dealing with Ireland and Greece, but the strategy is untenable in the longer term; a programme of open-ended bailouts is deeply unpopular in Germany and France, while the austerity measures designed to end the need for external loans have been met with protests in debtor states. Given current conditions, even with Greece's "haircut" of its debt in early 2012, it is probably futile to hope that indebted countries will eventually become solvent, or that Europe's debt crisis will abate in the absence of structural reforms or sovereign default. Moreover, endless bailouts would set the precedent that southern European countries can amass massive debts at the expense of the prudent North, which would only further alienate electors and corporations in countries such as Germany where the crisis has not been as protracted.

There are also the social and political ramifications throughout Greece and the rest of the Europe for the lack of economic growth and forced austerity measures. The public response to austerity measure and anaemic growth has been to turn to increasingly radical parties. Indeed, in Greece the election of SYRIZA—a communist party—in 2015 was supposed to bring about the end of the austerity. However, despite the promises of the Tsipras government, Greece was unable to negotiate more favourable terms from the "Troika" of the IMF, ECB and EC even after the 61% of the people of Greece voted against a new bailout package (Endghal 2015). The popular movement against austerity was shown to be insufficient compared to the capacity of foreign lenders to cut off Greece from European financial markets. The Tsipras government, despite popular rhetoric and the support from a majority of the people of Greece were unable to fundamentally change the terms of negotiations of the 2015 bailout package. The troika had too much leverage and institutional strength for Greece to negotiate an alternative to continued loans for austerity measures.

The socio-economic factors that led to the rise of SYRIZA should not be ignored. The long-term economic crisis in Greece after the onset of the recession was met with stringent austerity measures as a condition for loans. This crisis, however, has had dire social ramifications on the Greek people. SYRIZA and racialism within Greece, including the neo-fascist Golden Dawn, represent a broader populism, and disillusionment, with European institutions and "elites" (Stavrakakis and Katsambekis 2014). This populism usually stems from right-wing parties throughout Europe, but in the case of Greece, the left has been its main beneficiary. What the rise of these parties represents, even if they cannot negotiate successfully with the troika, is a schism between the views of many voters and the interests and demands of the so-called elites in European institutions. While it may be tempting to dismiss the Tsipras government as the exception, given the context, it represents a failure for conventional liberal parties to maintain control of the domestic political establishment within Greece. Furthermore, the scepticism of the people of Greece with their government and European institutions has become commonplace throughout Europe with the rise of populist movements.

Even with the crisis temporarily abated, a scenario facing European states is a major restructuring of the Eurozone, which may end with several countries being forced to abandon the common currency. Such a retrenchment would recognize that the structure of the system is unworkable and leads to the stronger countries retaining the Euro and the weaker economies reverting to their old national currencies. At first glance, this scenario may not seem overly likely, since the mere mention of Greece leaving the Eurozone can spark fears about capital flight that will threaten the overall economic stability of the EU.[7] As in the case of sovereign defaults, European leaders do not want to set the precedent that members can leave the Eurozone, particularly since there is no established method for a state to return its traditional currency.[8] Nonetheless, if Greece is forced to leave the union or leaves of its own volition, and the other PIIGS start to consider default as well, there will be intense pressure brought to bear on policy-makers to drastically restructure the Eurozone, which can only undermine the EU's long-term goal of continental integration. Even in the event that the Eurozone remains intact, European leaders will be left with a financially weakened institution suffering from severe internal cleavages between its members. At the same time, since the economic prospects for the Europe Union remain so dim, it is unlikely that its member-states will be able to overcome their looming social, demographic and security challenges.

A solution to this crisis proposed in November of 2011 was for fiscal integration of the European economies in exchange for liquidity injections from the ECB. This measure was introduced after Italian bond yields rose to an unsustainable level with many leaders worried the country was far too large and in debt to bail out should investors lose faith in Italian bonds. The fiscal union is intended to ensure greater stability from some of the weaker southern economies through stringent fiscal regulations and new austerity measures.[9] The purpose of this union is to provide money from Germany through the ECB to buy bonds in order to stabilize the PIIGS. In return, southern European countries lose a degree of fiscal autonomy through oversight over their budgets by limiting deficits to 0.5% of GDP.[10] This proposal will limit the growth of government programs by placing budgetary oversight in the hands of the European Commission instead of national legislatures. Ideally, this stipulation is intended to ease investor confidence by ensuring a restricted role for governments in their economies. Even in good times, but particularly during recessions, this is an extremely stringent limitation on the ability of governments to introduce fiscal stimulus. The intent of the union is to keep governments in future from too much intervention in their economies regardless of the circumstances or the demands of the public.

There are several obvious political issues with the proposed union. To begin with, the UK has vetoed its participation in this union—it does not want the financial centre of London to have to comply with far more stringent continental standards, nor does it want to pay a proposed financial transaction tax.[11] London has long been an international financial centre and does not want to invite competition from other cities. More substantively, the proposed fiscal union is wildly elitist and undemocratic. It takes away approval of national budgets from democratically elected legislatures and places it in the hands of technocrats at the EC. While the EU has traditionally been an elite-driven institution, this proposal will dramatically constrict national governments' intervention in their economies through extremely tight limits on deficit spending. Ironically, the outcome of the recession for the Euro—and saving the Eurozone— draws quite similar parallels to the gold standard in the 1930s. It is difficult and costly for countries to abandon the Euro for fear of capital flight and instability for the region, yet the austerity measures required to maintain the currency will lead to public outcry and will likely prolong the recession. And similar to the 1930s, without international leadership, the Europeans have elected to meet to demands of the financial system regardless of the consequences this will have on the public.

Moreover, the scepticism of the European Union is not limited to its members that are experiencing debt problems, the crisis of legitimacy has hindered the politics of its northern European members as well. In Great Britain, the UK Independence Party (UKIP) has increased its popular support in 2009 European parliament, despite finding itself unable to win seats in the British parliament the following year (Heyton 2010). While relatively small compared to other major parties in the UK, such as Labour and the Conservatives, UKIP has garnered the attention of the media and a core constituency of voters angry at the perceived injustice of the European Union, vowing "independence" from supposedly onerous European regulations and financial commitments. While initially it was assumed that the UK electoral system, First-Past-the-Post would "doom" the UKIP to being a largely irrelevant group unable to gain seats in parliament, its leader, Nigel Farage, turned out to be capable of building a sizable constituency for its views at the local level (Abdei and Lundburg 2009).

The popular support for UKIP in a series of local and European elections in Britain in 2014 had long-term political consequences for the UK and its place within the European Union. In the series of local elections in 2014, UKIP received 17% of the popular increased its number of seats and became the fourth largest party for local councils after Labour, the Tories and the Scottish National Party (Goodwin 2015). The local elections also coincided with elections to the European parliament. In this election with its proportional representation system, UKIP formed the largest group of MEPs, winning out over Labour and the Conservatives. This, of course, creates two problems: first, the largest group of elected officials representing the UK is actively opposed to the intrusion of the EU on British sovereignty; second, it creates an incentive for mainstream political parties to try to adopt some of the key policies of UKIP in order to attract some of their voters, particularly since the UK general election was to take place in 2015.

The sudden rise of UKIP left many in mainstream British parties afraid of a possible breakthrough of the party in the general election, particularly the governing Conservatives under the leadership of David Cameron. The British Conservatives have had a long-standing tradition of Euroscepticism, reluctant to join in Continental institutions and in the Euro currency. This tradition, along with pressure from UKIP and the Tory backbench, led Cameron to promise in 2013 a "yes or no" referendum on Britain remaining in the EU after the next election. This, of course, was a political tactic for Cameron in the lead up to the election in 2015. Cameron could ease the fears and anger from his caucus over Britain's role in the European Union, while also attracting supporters from UKIP, then after the election he could actively campaign to prevent the exit side from winning, leading to market instability and a political crisis within the UK.

The subsequent election in the UK led to a majority for the governing Conservatives, who had been part of a coalition government with the Liberal Democrats. The election proved to be disastrous for the opposition parties: the Labour vote increased but thanks to the popularity of the Scottish National Party in Scotland, Labour lost seats in parliament. The coalition partners of the Tories, the Liberal Democrats, had their vote collapse throughout the country, thereby losing their place in the coalition. Furthermore, contrary to the expectations of the UKIP making a breakthrough similar to those of the local elections, the party only attained a single seat in parliament despite receiving 12.7% of the popular vote. This result meant that the Cameron government would have little internal opposition to fulfil his promise to hold a referendum on Britain's continued presence in the European Union. In response to both winning a majority government and the policy as a main feature of the election platform of the Conservatives, David Cameron fulfilled his promise by setting up a referendum for the summer of 2016.

The so-called Brexit referendum created a schism within British political circles. On the "remain" side was the Prime Minister, a sizable portion of the Conservative caucus, the Opposition leader Jeremy Corbyn, most of Labour and the SNP, while the "leave" side was championed by Conservative MP Boris Johnson and Nigel Farage of UKIP. Along with its political infrastructure, the remain side had the support of academics and the financial industry from the City of London—they warned leaving the European Union would have a deleterious impact on the British economy and that Europe offered more benefits than costs (Jenson and Snaith 2016). The leave side emphasized the perceived costs of the European Union, as well as played upon the fear of immigrants and refugees, becoming a tone becoming commonplace among right-wing parties since the Syrian refugee crisis (Ibid). Initially, it appeared as though the remain side would win an easy victory, the popular support to remain seemed fairly consistent in polling. However, as the vote loomed, the race narrowed between the remain and leave sides, until on referendum day the leave side won a 51–48% margin (Surowiecki 2016) sending markets, and the British political establishment, into chaos.

The economic reaction from markets on the result of the Brexit vote was harsh and immediate. In response to the vote, the British Pound Sterling dropped to its lowest levels since 1987, even after recovering by mid-July of 2016, the Pound had declined in value compared to prior to the Brexit vote (Chu 2016). Moreover, the longer-term projections for Britain after it leaves the EU are even more troubling. By 2030, the GDP of Britain is projected to be lower by between 1.5 and 3.7% compared to baseline forecasts, with real wages falling by between 2.2 and 6.5% (Ebell and Warren 2016). The economy of the UK has become reliant upon the City of London and financial services. The Brexit vote could potentially harm Britain's access to the common European market—a necessity for a services-based economy. Furthermore, the decline of real wages will also harm the very people who voted in favour of leaving the European Union. The leave side often asserted that Britain was unfairly being constrained by European regulation and contributing more than it was receiving from the EU. Yet, the very people who voted in favour of leaving the EU, often older people from outside urban centres (Ibid), will feel a further decline in wages and economic opportunity as a result of Britain's exit from the European Union.

The economic crisis was temporarily abated by the resignation of David Cameron and his replacement by Theresa May, as well as a lack of pressure from the leave side to press the issue for a quick exit. Regardless of political postponements, both the EU and the Conservative caucus are aware they have to eventually turn the referendum outcome into tangible policy. The Conservative government is caught between several suboptimal options: either ignore the Brexit vote and find a way to avoid or ignore the issue altogether; face a backlash from the Conservative backbench and UKIP supporters who voted in for Brexit; present a renegotiation of the terms of the EU, which is by no means guaranteed since the EU will be party to the negotiations; or enact Article 50 and withdraw from the EU despite the considerable economic and political costs. In each of these circumstances, Britain faces considerable economic and political problems regardless of the choice of the British government; the project of a further integrated Europe, even among its northern European members, seems unlikely.

The Brexit vote has also raised concerns about the political unity of Britain and whether the country will be able to maintain its integrity. In the wake of the vote, leaders from the SNP and Northern Ireland, places where the remain side overwhelming won the vote, began openly discussing leaving the UK. Scotland, in particular, already held a referendum on whether to remain in the UK in 2014—which the "No" side to remain won by a margin of 55.3–44.7% (Hazell and Renwick 2016). If a hard Brexit occurs, and Britain is cut off from free travel and the common market, it could lead to a backlash from Scotland and Northern Ireland. Under these circumstances, if conditions were favourable, the SNP could call for a second referendum on independence and Sinn Fein could start negotiations to join with the Republic of Ireland (Ibid). Whether any of these scenarios actually come to pass is unclear, however, the Brexit vote has opened up a series of internal political issues that Britain did not face prior to the vote. It has exacerbated a schism between older voters and younger voters, England and Scotland and Northern Ireland, and between the financial interests and economic interests wanting access to Europe and nativist sentiments looking inwards.

The populist right-wing backlash against the displacement of economic globalization, the liberalization of finance and the integration of

Europe is occurring across the continent. Populist parties have become a prominent feature in countries as disparate as France, Hungary, Austria, Romania and Poland. Regardless of the specific national character of these movements, they share many of the same features: a scepticism of European integration, a resentment of the political establishment and a promise to shield the national "us" from the foreign "them" that seek to undermine economic prosperity (Rooduijn 2015). The popularity of these groups has been exacerbated by the dual problems of the Syrian refugee crisis and economic stagnation and decline in the aftermath of the Great Recession. These populist parties represent a constituency of voters that feel left behind by the European integration project. The supporters of right-wing nationalist movements often come from the traditional working class, whom have faced two pressures: from economic competition due to integration, but also from their cultural identity being threatened by immigrant communities (Oesch 2015). The promise of right-wing parties to protect cultural identity from fear of the other, more so than any specific economic grievance, particularly against the project of European integration, is one of the key reasons for their rise in support. Thus, rather than Britain's experience with Brexit and Greece's rise of radical parties, the phenomenon of nativist backlash in Europe is occurring across the continent.

The Rising Threat to American Hegemony?

The purpose of this chapter has been to evaluate the relative economic and political capabilities of an alternative global power: the European Union. In this, domestic political, economic or social problems will prevent both from challenging the USA as the dominant hegemonic power in the global capitalist system. For the countries tied to the Euro, the continuing debt crisis has bled into a political crisis, with leaders from Europe's south resenting the austerity measures demanded by politicians from Germany and France as a condition for loans. Since the post-war years, the European project has largely been an elite-driven process, one that hopes to bind Europe together both economically and politically. Now Europe is anything but unified. Many in the north of Europe, particularly in Germany, resent providing money for their southern counterparts. As a response, politicians in the South are seeking more radical alternatives, such as SYRIZA in Greece, a communist, anti-austerity party. In all regions of Europe, the prospect of further unifying

Europe into a more cohesive political union remains unlikely in the face of popular opposition, recession and demographic challenges.

Furthermore, the Eurozone has been mired in slow economic growth since 2009 and, even with a haircut on Greek debt activating its sovereign default swaps, the crisis has no spread beyond the continent. With the election of SYRIZA in 2015, there was even the notion of Greece leaving the Eurozone if it could not negotiate a better deal with its lenders. However, even with Greek voters rejecting the terms of the loans by major European countries, the Greek government, led by Alexis Tsipras, eventually capitulated, well aware that leaving the Eurozone would be even more catastrophic for the Greek economy than the austerity demanded by the Germans. Yet, despite these political and economic problems causing anaemic growth for the entire region, the rest of the global economy was more affected by a downturn in energy prices than problems in the Eurozone. Even in the North, the economic and political hub of Project Europe, there is discontent. In Britain, always reluctant of closer ties to the continent, the government is facing domestic and international divisions. Scotland held a referendum in 2014 over whether to separate from the UK. While the Scots voted to stay in the UK, the demands for greater autonomy within the union show that even countries with a relatively stable political system face internal divisions in face of recession and economic hardship. In the summer of 2016, Britain also voted in favour of a Brexit, leading to a political crisis within Britain's political class. With new found popularity of the British "going it alone", it does signify a worrying sign: European integration will be politically difficult in the UK for the foreseeable future, ensuring that the other major powers on the continent will not be able to rely upon London for support.

Thus far, I have highlighted the structural economic problems between the European North and South, the institutional problems within the European Union and the political backlash from Greece and Britain. Altogether, these factors make it unlikely further integration will be possible among European partners, let alone forming a union capable of becoming a counter-weight to American economic hegemony. These political problems within Europe are not easily mitigated given the longer-term demographic, social and political issues within Europe. Even with German leadership under Angela Merkel trying to keep the project together, she too faces a nativist backlash within Germany that could threaten her leadership. The future for the European Union as both an economic and political union looks bleak. Its regions are mired in recession and low growth, there is no consensus on moving the region towards a fiscal union, and its monetary union has experienced a series of crisis from its indebted southern members, and many of its keep core countries are facing the rise of right-wing populist parties or other anti-integration movements. While the European Union may survive these crises, for the time being, it is far from challenging the USA's dominance on a global level.

NOTES

1. Elliot Posner, "European approach to financial regulation," *Global Finance in Crisis*. Eds. Eric Helleiner, Stefano Pagliari, Hubert Zimmerman (Routledge, New York, 2010): 111.
2. Ibid., 118.
3. The Economist "The IMF, America and the Euro: sympathy but no money," *The Economist*. (4 November 2011): http://www.economist.com/blogs/charlemagne/2011/11/imf-america-and-euro.
4. Ibid.
5. The Economist, "The euro area's debt crisis," *The Economist*. (12 January 2011): http://www.economist.com/node/17902709
6. BBC Business News,"Euro falls on rumours Greece is to quit the Eurozone," *BBC News Magazine*, (May 7th, 2011): http://www.bbc.co.uk/news/business-13317770.
7. Larry Elliot, "Greece wouldn't find it easy to leave the euro," *The Guardian*, 20 April 2010, http://www.guardian.co.uk/world/2010/apr/29/greece-euro-debt-crisis.
8. Ibid.
9. Quentin Peel, "Eurozone set for Fiscal Union, Says Merkel," *Financial Times*. (December 14th 2011).
10. Ibid.
11. Ibid.

CHAPTER 5

The Demographic and Economic Problems of China

On the surface, it seems as though the Chinese economy has come through the recession relatively unscathed. One of the key assumptions of the International Relations literature is that as countries become more powerful, both in terms of economics and military might, they will start to displace the pre-existing world order (Christensen and Xing 2016). China's dramatic rise since the 2000s, along with America's foreign policy problems and the Great Recession, could further contribute to its challenge to the hegemony of the USA. Yet the financial crisis has highlighted numerous potential problems that could undermine its economic growth and stability. The country has become too reliant upon American consumption for economic growth. The massive investment in US debt kept Americans buying Chinese goods throughout the 2000s, and another downturn in the USA could have significant repercussions for the regime. In America, it has also led to a contradiction between those in defence and in business. China is viewed as a major security threat by the defence establishment, yet business and the US economy are reliant upon its cheap labour. However, beneath the ostensibly stable face of the regime, there are signs of internal weakness in the Chinese economy, particularly in its housing market and stock market, and dissatisfaction among its populace. China was often lauded during the recession for having a stable economic and for its economic growth, yet it appears to be facing a problem commonplace in middle-income countries: transition to a high income country without undermining the regime's hold on power. Unlike Europe and USA

© The Author(s) 2018
B. Tozzo, *American Hegemony after the Great Recession*, International Political Economy Series, https://doi.org/10.1057/978-1-137-57539-5_5

where citizens have the capacity to air their grievances through elections and referenda, China has an authoritarian regime. Furthermore, since the Great Recession, China's seemingly stable economy and internal drive to "go global" have been wrought with internal political strife and economic hardship (Shambaugh 2013). An economic crisis in China has the potential to undermine the regime and could have dire consequences for the rest of the global economy. As a possible contender to compete with American hegemony, China has numerous demographic, political and economic issues.

CRISIS IN THE WEST, OPPORTUNITY FOR CHINA?

China has certainly achieved an impressive level of economic growth since opening its economy to foreign investment in the late 1970s. The recession in China was neither as protracted nor as deep as it was in America and Europe. It still had a significant drop in trade due to the collapse in demand from its largest exporters, but it quickly rebounded due to a rapid and well financed stimulus package and relatively diversified trade.[1] Also, China has been a major financier of American deficit spending since the start of the crisis, allowing the Americans to spend at low interest rates. Many scholars from both the mainstream literature such as Niall Ferguson and the critical literature such as Giovanni Arrighi have even predicted the twenty-first century will see China arise as the new hegemon.[2] Of course, it is beyond the parameters of this book predict the future of the international system. However, contrary to the expectations of Arrighi, several domestic and international problems could inhibit China's ascent. Though Beijing has built institutional and economic barriers to prevent a similar financial catastrophe that struck the USA and Europe, there are numerous potential weaknesses in the Chinese economic model that make it susceptible to fluctuations. There are also several looming demographic and social problems that could derail China's continued economic development.

China's sheer economic growth and financial resources over the past few decades have been impressive, however, since the recession, its economic model has started to show its flaws. In comparison to New York or London, government bureaucrats have a high degree of oversight over China's financial system. The Chinese Communist Party (CCP) through the People's Bank of China has a dominant presence in China's banking sector and can target investment, even foreign investment, to meet political and policy objectives.³ This system has obvious advantages: it provides government resources to undertake large projects that private investors may be unwilling to finance. It has been under close government scrutiny that development has taken place. However, the system has numerous flaws. The Chinese government is prone to factionalism where investments are made for political reasons to maximize the power of one faction over another.⁴ Due to the secrecy of China's government, this has led many analysts to estimate there may be billions worth of bad loans which in the aggregate could inhibit China's future growth.⁵ So although the oversight of the government in China's financial system makes it less sensitive to the fluctuations of a private market, the system is prone to corruption due to factional infighting from the CCP.

Despite considerable improvements in living standards, China remains a poor country that must grapple with a range of domestic and regional challenges before it can hope to compete with America for pre-eminence. Even after two decades of exponential growth, the Chinese economy is still less than one-third of the size of its American counterpart,⁶ despite the fact that China's population is over four times larger than that of the USA. In China, domestic challenges have taken the form of a series of social pathologies that include rampant inequality, a greying population and an unbalanced gender ratio. Even though China has had an impressive level of economic growth in recent years, it must be kept in mind that, despite its growing prosperity, it is still a very poor country. In 2010, the per capita income in China is only USD $7600 (PPP) per year, lower than Jamaica or Albania.⁷ In addition, the distribution of this newfound wealth is incredibly uneven. In 2010, the average rural income was in China only $935 (PPP) per year, while urban workers have an annual income of $2965 (PPP), more than three times as much as their rural counterparts.⁸ Even if entrepreneurs are making millions from China's rapid development, the bulk of China's workforce remains poor, especially in the countryside. In fact, the high level of economic inequality between rural and urban workers has led to concern that the Chinese economy is becoming "Latin Americanized", or extremely economically unequal.

As part of its efforts to tackle these problems, Beijing has begun to undertake reforms to lower education costs and increase the amount of low-income housing, but these policies are proving expensive, particularly in light of its rapidly greying population.⁹ It is estimated that by 2020, one in five people in China will be over the age of 65, placing further pressure on its old-age pension program already viewed as inadequate in many rural regions of the country.[10] By 2050, the median age in China will be 45, and over a third of the Chinese population will over 60 years of age. Even if China can maintain its impressive growth rates, which is by no means assured, the Chinese government will still face enormous challenges providing services to a population that is growing older and more unequal.

In addition to the problems posed by inequality and an ageing population, in the next few decades, China will face a devastating demographic crisis due to the retention of the "family planning policy", put in place in 1978 to curb massive population growth by restricting the number of children born to urban families. While the one child policy has been successful in limiting population growth, it has had the unintended effect of creating an increasingly large disparity between males and females, as Chinese parents have demonstrated a marked willingness to abort or abandon unwanted girls. Most countries possess a gender ratio of 103–107 males for every 100 females, in China the gender gap was already 119 men for every 100 women in 2005. If these trends continue, this will lead to 40 million more men than women by 2020,[11] and anywhere from 17 to 42 million more adult men than women by 2050.[12] There can be little doubt that the high gender imbalance will create a massive strain on the social order, since less wealthy men will be unable to marry and have children, creating a large underclass of poor, low-status males who are unable to find wives. Research conducted in this area has shown that unmarried, economically disadvantaged men tend to commit more violent crime and are more likely to join radical militant movements,[13] and China's skewed demographic ratio is likely to result in a large pool of frustrated and disenfranchised males. Thus, in coming decades, China will be forced to cope with a population of millions of adult men with little wealth and no stake in the existing order, which will undoubtedly place a significant strain on the resources of the Chinese government as it attempts to maintain order and facilitate economic growth.

So far, China's high level of economic growth has meant that widening social cleavages have not presented a serious threat to the rule of the CCP, which has managed to bolster its legitimacy by positioning itself as a regime capable of delivering prosperity to its people.[14] However, it must be kept in mind that China's developmental model is predicated on economic growth and positive relations with the USA, the country that its rise is supposedly threatening to unseat as hegemon of the international system. Despite the global economic downturn, the USA remains China's most important export market, making up close to 20% of China's foreign trade in 2010.[15] There are two major reasons why this is the case. The first has to do with the value of the Renminbi vis-à-vis the US dollar. By comparative standards, China's currency is pegged well below its US counterpart, providing an immediate economic incentive to American consumers to buy Chinese goods. The second has to do with the low wages paid to Chinese workers. Although the wages of China's urban workforce have increased over the past decade, they still remain extremely low by American standards. These low wages decrease production costs, which further lowers the price of goods and encourages US consumption.[16] As a result of these factors, Washington has been placing pressure on China to revalue the Renminbi, arguing that it provides an unfair advantage to Chinese producers while at the same time hindering domestic production and consumption.[17] Beijing's resistance to this pressure stems from its fear that increasing the value of the Renminbi too rapidly could serve as a disincentive for investment, slowing exports to the USA and leading to unemployment to China. Since a major downturn in the economy could lead to protests and riots against the ruling party, as well as reducing the resources available for programs designed alleviate China's social ills, the Chinese government remains dependent on US consumer demand in order to provide the prosperity that it uses to justify its rule.

One consequence of China's reliance on American consumption to ensure its own economic prosperity has been willingness of the Chinese government to invest heavily in US debt. Throughout the 2000s, Americans were able to borrow massive sums of money at low interest rates without having to worry about a negative reaction from financial markets, and much of that money was provided by Chinese banks. The Chinese were willing to invest in American debt for a number of reasons, the most important being that US Treasury bonds were seen as a safe investment, but also because buying up these assets allowed American consumers to keep spending money on Chinese goods. The trillion dollar obligation the US owes the Chinese places Washington in a weakened position, and on the surface, it does seem as if China holds a great deal of economic leverage over the USA.

However, China's vast exposure to American debt is a double-edged sword. The Chinese are *too* invested in the USA to withdraw their financing, which in turn decreases any leverage Beijing might have over American economic policy. This reason behind this entrapment has to do with several important pathologies of Chinese development. State-owned enterprises continue to be a key component of China's domestic economy; they depend upon growth in China's privately owned foreign investment for growth and profitability (Vermieren 2014). This has led to a broad penetration of the use of fixed assets in both state-owned enterprises and in private enterprises that rely upon exports (Ibid 2014). Deleveraging itself from the USA would be difficult. Even if the government slowly started selling off Treasury bonds, it would shake the confidence of international investors, leading to an increase in interest rates as the USA struggled to finance its deficit and avoid default.[18] Higher interest rates would also slow US consumer spending, hurting Chinese exports and its state-owned enterprises and leading to unemployment as factories close and workers are laid off. In addition to the domestic repercussions, any remaining US debt held by the Chinese government would decline in value, since it would become harder to sell off bonds as US interest rates rose. China's economic future is therefore tightly bound to that of America, since any action that undermined the US economy would have dire consequences for the Chinese economy as well.

Also, China has not completely insulated itself from domestic and international economic turmoil. It has started to reach a development plateau with its low-wage workforce requiring higher value-added industries in order to keep up its economic growth.[19] Similar to other Asian countries, China must diversify its economic and political system if it wants to continue to develop. This does not suggest China will democratize in the near future, however, China's continued development requires increasing the value of the Renminbi to lower the cost of purchasing foreign technology and reducing the intervention of the Chinese government in order to better meet domestic and foreign consumer demand.[20] Thus far, the CCP has been willing to gradually increase the Renminbi but has been far more reluctant to withdraw its control from the economy—a testament to a regime that is highly self-conscious. Though China's growth since 2008 had been mainly due to domestic consumption, there are limits on how protracted this recovery can be if the EU and America fall back into recession. Despite a burgeoning middle class, China still relies on foreign exports in order to keep its job market growing. If another major financial crisis hits a major trading partner, despite the resources of the CCP, it could hamper China's economic growth.

There are also fears China could experience a housing market collapse similar to the USA and Europe. Since the crisis occurred in 2008, the CCP introduced a series of stimulus measures coupled with low interest rates on loans from Chinese banks.[21] The intent of these policies was to prevent a protracted economic recession from threatening China's growth and ipso facto the legitimacy of the regime. Similar to the USA in the early 2000s, many Chinese people took out cheap loans and began to speculate on the value of their property.[22] This has led to a housing market boom in areas of China, but has led many to worry that a collapse of the market may harm the Chinese economy. The government has begun to raise interest rates to lower demand, but a correction in the value of the market of this scale could represent the loss of the billions in equity for many Chinese people. While China's banks have considerable government oversight—preventing a similar bankruptcy to Lehman Brothers in the USA—there is potential for a major recession to hit the Chinese economy. So, despite its institutional barriers in place by the CCP, the liberalization of the economy has made China vulnerable to financial markets. This could have massive potential consequences on the stability of the Chinese regime and on global economic stability.

More recently, China's economy has experienced a stock market crisis in 2015, though this has not translated into a broader economic downturn in the economy. There is, of course, some difficulty in relying upon government-based reports, since the government has a political incentive to promote data favourable to the regime. Nonetheless, despite the lack of reliable information there has been a slowdown in private-sector investment, from growth of more than 40% in 2011 to just 2.8% in the first half of 2016 (Economist 2016). Rather than an anomaly, the lack of private-sector investment is indicative of other worrying signs in the economy. Although the Chinese economy is still growing, there are other sign of underlying economic strain. The credit market in China is on a sharp increase compared to nominal growth, growing at 16% this year, meaning loose monetary policy set by the central bank is allowing for both private and state-owned enterprises to leverage at a rapid pace. Moreover, China's debt-to-GDP level has exploded—from roughly 150% before the 2008 global financial crisis to more than 250% in 2016 (Economist 2016). This puts it similar to countries such as Spain and Japan, both have long-term structural economic problems that will undermine growth for the foreseeable future. In a period of eight years since the onset of the financial crisis, China has gone from a country that was praised for its resilience, to one of the most in debt large economies in the world. While it would be premature to suggest China will face similar economic problems, the sheer amount of debt in China has led the IMF to publish a working paper on how to ease China's debt problems before they lead to a crisis that will affect the domestic and international economy.

The IMF report identified several measures to ease China's debt burden and aid its economy to transition from a middle-income country to a higher income country. The paramount recommendation is that the Chinese government must recognize and cease supporting, through favourable loans and government-backing, failing and bankrupt companies (IMF 2016). The Chinese government has long protected industries that have close ties to the party. Though there has been a recognition by the Chinese government to tackle corruption within state-owned enterprises, there is still a reluctance by officials to let companies go bankrupt if they face significant economic problems. There is excessive corporate debt and a reluctance among the political establishment to lift the implicit guarantees on SOEs and make the necessary structural changes to reform China's economy including the privatization of telecommunications and energy sectors (Economist 2016). While these economic recommendations may be necessary to avoid a crisis in China's economy by providing some "short-term pain for long-term gain", the political will to implement them is lacking (IMF 2016). There is a reluctance within the Chinese political establishment to accept policies that may undermine economic growth for fear of causing political strife in the country, even if in the long-term it may be beneficial to the country.

These economic problems have not gone unnoticed by the people of China—there has been an exponential increase in the quality and quantity of strikes and protests from Chinese workers and social groups. As economic growth has slowed, wages and job growth have declined as well—many workers have been denied wages, leading to strikes and labour protests erupting across the country (Hernandez 2016). A labour rights group based in Hong Kong—the Chinese Labour Bulletin—recorded more than 2700 strikes and protests in 2015, more than double the number in 2014; the strife appears to have intensified in the early months of 2016, with more than 500 protests in January alone (Ibid). Yet again, we get a significant tension between the top-down policy from the Chinese government and the response from people who are faced with precarious working conditions and less pay. If the Chinese government does implement structural reform to the economy, it will lead to the failure of many SOEs that have been propped up through favourable conditions by the Chinese government. However, if they are allowed to fail, more protests with erupt from angry workers who are either unemployed or must continue to accept less wages.

Despite the sophisticated mechanisms for repression from the Chinese government, the protests are becoming increasingly better organized and sophisticated. Since protests have become widespread, protesters have been using social media as an organizational tool (Minter 2016). The response of the Chinese government to these protests across state-owned and private enterprises has been the same: to arrest dissidents, clamp down on social media and delete news reports on strikes (Ibid). In particular, the Chinese government has devoted more resources to limiting social media and quickly deleting protests and anti-government riots from dissenting workers. The Chinese government has a long-standing policy to block platforms that may be used to organize dissent or spread messages that threaten its legitimacy. For example, some of the largest social media sites used in the West, like Facebook and Twitter, have been blocked by the Chinese government and politically sensitive phrases are often quickly deleted from blogs and other websites (Bamman 2012). Even with these obvious impediments, labour groups use social media platforms to organize and spread their discontent. Some of the largest and well-organized protests, typically numbering in the thousands though difficult to confirm, have come from China's north-eastern state-owned coal industry, which has been hit by the slowing of the Chinese economy. The demands of the workers are commonplace payment of wages and better working conditions. However, the state-owned coal industry is caught in a bind: demand for coal has declined by 6% in 2015, while the industry must provide the supply at below market prices to keep energy prices low for other Chinese industries and for growing cities (Hornby 2016).

The case of the coal worker strike highlights a growing tension within China: between the economic restructuring that is necessary to prevent a widespread recession throughout the country and the expedient political and economic policies that maintain control for the Communist Party. Indeed, the crackdown on worker protests and censorship is not a sign of strength, but speaks to the fragility of the regime:

Despite appearances, China's political system is badly broken, and nobody knows it better than the Communist Party itself. China's strongman leader, Xi Jinping, is hoping that a crackdown on dissent and corruption will shore up the party's rule. He is determined to avoid becoming the Mikhail Gorbachev of China, presiding over the party's collapse. But instead of being the antithesis of Mr. Gorbachev, Mr. Xi may well wind up having the same effect. His despotism is severely stressing China's system and society—and bringing it closer to a breaking point. (Shambaugh 2015: 2)

The actions of the Chinese party against dissent are not a testament to its power, but a sign of its weakness. Unlike democratic countries, where people can voice their dissent and periodically vote their leaders out, the Chinese government is unwilling to tolerate political opposition to the regime. While the methods to combat protesters are getting more sophisticated, every time the Chinese government intervenes, it shows the vulnerability of the government: it is a self-conscious regime that is aware that its own legitimacy may be threatened. The actions of the business elite in China are another sign of discontent with the regime: 64% of 393 millionaires and billionaires polled by the Hurun Research Institute are currently emigrating or planning to leave China, and they are sending their children to study abroad (Shambaugh 2015). While it is far too premature to tell if the regime is threatened, the protests from industrial workers and the reluctance of elites to commit to the country's future offer worrying signs for the regime.

Moreover, China's rapid development has not gone unnoticed by the American security establishment. Currently, two contradictory streams of thought about the relative rise of China are common among Washington policy-makers. First is that a prosperous China will be a positive outcome for regional and global security and development.[23] Some policy-makers argue China has already integrated peacefully into the international institutions and a wealthier China could be a large market for imports from the USA. Thus far, at least, Beijing has been relatively accommodating to Western interests and open to Western investment. Even when tension has occurred in the past, such as when the Americans bombed a Chinese embassy in Kosovo, the close economic ties have been a stabilizing force in China's relationship to the West.[24] Thus China's ascent could be peaceful if both sides are willing to continue compromising on economic and security matters. Indeed, thus far, the relationship between China and the USA has been called "interdependent hegemony": the two powers have built a political and economic framework that provides accommodation and integrates China into the pre-existing hegemonic system where conflict can be resolved through institutional channels (Christensen and Xing 2016).

On the other hand, some in the security establishment believe it is only a matter of time before China becomes more assertive over Taiwan and scarce oil and other natural resources.[25] They argue a rising China will displace the contemporary balance of power and instigate conflict with the USA. The past may not be indicative of the future and China is facing a series of domestic and international challenges moving from a middle-income to high income country. Also due to US pressure, China is facing growing pressure to realign its currency, a greater number of trade investment and intellectual property disputes, a more hostile security environment and exclusionary regional trans-Pacific and trans-Atlantic trade agreements, such as the Trans-Pacific Partnership (Glenn 2017). While US–China relations have been relatively stable for the past 40 years, it is not necessarily an indication that they will remain so inevitably as China continues to grow as a global power and the USA becomes more protectionist. With recent historical examples such as the ascent of Germany leading to the two world wars or the Soviet Union's 50-year Cold War, they argue Washington should take precautions over a rapidly developing China. These policy-makers advocate heightened preparedness with increased military spending and stronger ties to allies in Southeast Asia.[26] Washington should not be reluctant to take a hard line to defend its economic and security interests when they will be, inevitably, threatened by Beijing.

This has led to a contradiction between those in the security establishment and those in the economic and business community. China is both a potential threat and a potential stabilizing force. As discussed earlier, China and the USA are highly interdependent with the Chinese holding trillions in US debt while relying upon the Americans to consume Chinese-made products. Many realists often point out Europe was highly integrated prior to the First World War, particularly Britain and Germany, but this did not prevent a catastrophic conflict from engulfing the continent.[27] This ignores the fact many European leaders believed the war would be short and inexpensive, and not a long, protracted, violent affair that left millions dead and four empires in ruins.[28] The war also displaced international economic integration for the next 50 years—not exactly a predictable outcome from a conflict that was supposed to be over by the Christmas of 1914. Few, if any, scholars or policy-makers are under the illusion that a conflict between China and the America would be cheap in terms of materiel or human lives or easily resolvable once started. Both Beijing and Washington recognize their mutual economic reliance and the advent of nuclear weapons, perhaps a key reason the Cold War did not cascade into a full out war, raises the costs of great power conflict even further. Yet, many in Washington still view China as threat to American interests.

While seemingly unaffected by the financial crisis, by 2015, China began to experience an economic downturn of its own. In many ways, China is a victim of its own economic model. Its stock market, which continued to grow after many in the West were mired in recession, experienced a rapid decline in the summer of 2015, losing almost $5 trillion in value. While stock markets are not the only, or even the best, test of a country's economic vitality, there are other worrying signs China may be in for a difficult period. The very industrial process behind China's economic development—manufacturing goods for export—is being adopted by other countries in the region with cheaper labour markets, such as Vietnam. Though China is still a strong regional power, it seems to be experiencing a middle-income country trap. It is finding the transition from middle-income status to high income, difficult for a series of international and domestic economic problems.

The rise of China could lead to tension with the USA, but conflict between these two countries would have dire economic consequences for the global economy. It is possible that domestic or international factors could lead Beijing to be more aggressive on issues such as Taiwan leading to a direct confrontation with the USA, but if the economic consequences of 9/11 or the financial crisis are any indication, financial markets will limit the policies of these countries. Both countries are reliant upon the free mobility of goods and finance to maintain economic growth and prosperity. In China's case, the regime depends on job creation for stability. The international economy in this case has conditioned the two countries to, at least thus far, peacefully co-exist with each other, with neither country willing to destabilize the global economy. Financial markets have the capacity to punish countries for acting contrary to the demands of capital and the USA and China are no exception.

Even with a downturn in China's stock market, the American economy is projected to grow at almost 3% due to cheaper energy and its economy finally coming out of recession. While broader economic instability could potentially have reverberations in the USA, or in other regions where the Chinese government has made investments, for the time being the American economic recovery is proceeding despite problems with one of its largest trading partners. However, China's economic problems remain both political and economic problems for China. It is a political problem for the Chinese government because its legitimacy is derived largely from its ability to provide economic returns to its people. If it enters a period of poor growth, its political leaders could face pressure both from within the Communist party and from the public. Unlike democracies, there is no formal institutional mechanism for the public to voice its dissent. However, even with China's ascent as a global economic superpower, its economic problems seem to be isolated within China and have not led to a broader global crisis in capitalism. As I will discuss in the next chapter, the most significant threat to the global economy is from the very country at the hub of the global financial system: the USA.

NOTES

1. Jonathan Eaton, Samuel Kortum, Brent Neiman and John Romalis "Trade and the Global Recession". *The National Bureau of Economic Research*. Working Paper No. 16666, (January 2011): 1.
2. Niall Ferguson, *Civilization: The West and the Rest* (The Penguin Press, New York, 2011); Arrighi, *Adam Smith in Beijing*.
3. Victor C Shih. *Factions and Finance in China* (Cambridge MA, Cambridge University Press, 2008): 3
4. Ibid., 4.
5. Ibid., 4.
6. The World Bank estimates China's nominal GDP at $4.5 trillion, making it a fraction of America's $14.1 trillion annual output, CIA Worldfactbook, Country Comparison: GDP—per capita (PPP), *Central Intelligence Agency*. Washington, D.C. (July 2010): https://www.cia.gov/library/publications/the-world-factbook/rankorder/2004rank.html?countryName=China&countryCode=ch&regionCode=eas&rank=126#ch.
7. Ibid.
8. Dexter Roberts, "China's Growing Income Gap," *Bloomberg Businessweek*, (27 January 2011): http://www.businessweek.com/magazine/content/11_06/b4214013648109.htm.
9. Ibid.
10. Wang Dewen, "China's Urban and Rural Old Age Security System: Challenges and Options". *China & World Economy*. Vol. 14, No. 1, (February 2006): 102.

11. The Telegraph, "Chinese gender imbalance will leave millions of men without wives". *The Telegraph*, (11 January 2011), http://www.telegraph.co.uk/news/worldnews/asia/china/6966037/Chinese-gender-imbalance-will-leave-millions-of-men-without-wives.html.
12. Isabelle Attané "The Demographic Impact of a Female Deficit in China, 2000–2050". Population and Development Review, Vol. 32, No. 4, (December 2006): 767.
13. Therese Hesketh and Zhu Wei Xing, "Abnormal sex ratios in human populations: Causes and consequences". Proceedings of the National Academy of Science, Vol. 103, No. 36, (September 2006): 13271.
14. The Economist, "Fear of the Dragon," *The Economist*. (7 January 2010), http://www.economist.com/node/15235078?Story_ID=E1_TVNPVDSR.
15. Ibid.
16. The Economist, "China's Tricky Wage Dynamics," *The Economist*. (5 April 2011), http://www.economist.com/blogs/freeexchange/2011/04/labour_markets_0.
17. Ibid.
18. Bill Gertz "Chinese see U.S. debt as weapon in Taiwan dispute," *The Washington Post*, (10 February 2010): http://www.washingtontimes.com/news/2010/feb/10/chinese-see-us-debt-as-weapon/.
19. William Overholt "China in the Global Financial Crisis: Rising Influence, Rising Challenges" *Washington Quarterly*. Vol. 33, No. 1. (January 2010): 26.
20. Ibid.
21. Jamil Anderlini "Chinese property: a lofty ceiling," *The Financial Times*. (31 December 2011).
22. Ibid.
23. Thomas J. Christensen "Fostering Stability or Creating a Monster? The Rise of China and U.S. Policy toward East Asia," *International Security*. Vol. 31, No. 1, (Summer 2006): 81.
24. Aaron L. Friedberg "The Future of U.S.-China Relations: Is Conflict Inevitable?" *International Security*. Vol. 30, No. 2, (Fall 2005,): 8. (7–45).
25. Christensen, 81.
26. Friedberg, 8.
27. Dale C. Copeland, "Economic Interdependence and War: A Theory of Trade Expectations," *International Security*, Vol. 20, No. 4 (Spring 1996). 21.
28. Ibid.

CHAPTER 6

American Political Polarization and the Rise of Trump

This chapter will continue the analysis started in Chap. 3 by examining the events leading up to the Great Recession and the polarization that has hampered the American political response to the crisis since the 2010 midterm elections. The weakness in the American economy led to a global financial crisis in 2008 and the subsequent Great Recession. The crisis spread throughout the global economy, yet the recession is not a uniform problem: its characteristics vary with a specific region's economy, politics, culture and institutions. I will show how the Great Recession is both parts of the same global crisis in capitalism and a series of local crises. In America to reform finance, Obama proposed new regulations for the global economy in order to prevent another major downturn. However, the response of the Obama administration has been complicated by polarization of American politics. The bailout of the financial system has been contested by the Tea Party on the right and the Occupy Wall Street movement on the left. These social movements along with America's divided government have hampered its ability to deal with domestic economic issues, as well as its capacity to take a leadership role in order to mitigate the broader global crisis.

Critical theories tend to argue American policy is dictated by the demands of the capitalist system, whether it be corporations or financial markets. I will provide an analysis of these events by examining a complex series of determinants of American policy and global finance. A major theme of this chapter will be the spatial displacement due to the recent contradictions in capitalism. With the financial crisis of 2008, the

© The Author(s) 2018 93
B. Tozzo, *American Hegemony after the Great Recession*, International Political Economy Series, https://doi.org/10.1057/978-1-137-57539-5_6

neoliberal agenda that America had been central in promoting throughout the twentieth century began to harm the economy of the USA. The election of Barack Obama led many scholars and journalists to hope the USA could resolve the tensions with the financial system. They hoped the Obama administration would be able to manage the recession, which started as one of the largest downturns in the American economy since the 1930s.

Yet despite Obama's presidency little has changed: the USA still regularly intervenes in the Middle East, and despite the several stimulus packages, several rounds of Quantitative Easing, America's economic future remains uncertain among the population. The gradual deregulation of the financial system over the past 40 years provided private investors the ability to condition both the US government and the international banking system, limiting the options for the Obama administration. While the crisis itself was brought about by the bankruptcy of Lehman Brothers, the role of derivatives, and a failing mortgage market, the determinants of the recession have deeper historical roots. By the time the financial crisis hit, America alone could not, and cannot, manage the financial system. Although the crisis and the recession started under the presidency of George W. Bush, the recession has shaped the policies of Barack Obama. Indeed, there has been a remarkable continuity between these two administrations. This is due to politics, on the one hand, forcing Washington to enact policies that are popular on the home front, and through international financial markets, on the other, constraining the options for the American government. The central thesis of this is that, despite the economic pressures and contradictions of the international financial system, the main threat to the stability of the capitalist system is the inability of the American government to manage crisis due to its polarized and ineffectual political system. To explore this, I will examine the immediate response of the American government to financial crisis through its haphazard response to the bankruptcies of Lehman Brothers, the failure to pass a bailout package of the banking system, the continual problem to pass a budget and coming within hours of failing to pass the debt ceiling—an arbitrary limit on government debt—on several occasions. The polarization of the American political system is nothing new, of course. The system was polarized between Federalists and Anti-Federalists shortly after its inception, and the divisions caused by slavery led to the American civil war. In the twentieth century, Americans were divided on whether to participate in the world wars, whether to institute social programs, and on civil rights. However, as I will discuss, the most recent iteration of polarization in its political system has significant consequences for the American and international economy—one that could undermine America's position as hegemon and the stability of the global capitalist system. The most striking internal threat to American hegemony has been with Donald Trump winning the Republican nomination and the presidency in 2016. Rather than an exception, Trump's platform is the culmination of many long-standing pathologies within American politics, fuelled by populist resentment at the economic displacement in the wake of the Great Recession.

THE GREAT RECESSION AND AMERICAN POLITICAL CONFLICT

The Great Recession has led many scholars to question the hegemony of the USA, which was at the centre of the crisis. Since the 1980s, the American government has promoted the financialization of both the US and global economy. Financing was used to overcome barriers to accumulation, opening up new untapped markets for profit. In the USA, lax credit requirements integrated lower income Americans into the financial system. Meanwhile, the savings of people in China was used to keep interest rates in the USA low, perpetuating a credit bubble by linking American consumers to the Chinese economy (Panitch and Konings 2009). When periodic crises occurred prior 2008, it was usually in emerging economies, such as South America in the 1980s and Southeast Asia in the 1990s. The subprime mortgage crisis of 2008 showed the USA was just as vulnerable to global finance as any other economy. Moreover, America was the hub of a financial system, so the contagion quickly spread to Europe and Asia becoming a truly global financial crisis.

The financial crisis cannot be understood without a broader understanding of the global expansion of capitalism in South Asia, the complexity of the financial system, and the specifics of the American housing market. As discussed in Chap. 2, neoliberalism arose out of the contradictions in the post-war consensus. After the collapse of the Soviet Union and the opening of China, there were fewer international barriers to investment and profit. The reduction of these barriers led to an explosion of global investment capital, particularly in East Asia. However, along with the growth in scope of the financial system, its ability to rapidly undermine the strength of an economy also grew as discussed previously with the 1997 Asian Financial Crisis. Yet, when periodic crises occurred, the American government was available to provide assistance and prevent a broader downturn in the global economy. Prior to 2008, it seemed as though major developed countries benefited from the financialization of markets, with the USA retaining its status of hegemon for nearly two decades after the fall of the USSR. Yet, the very method for prolonging America's dominance through the liberalization of finance led to a contradiction in the global economy in 2008, with the USA at the centre.

With trillions of dollars moving around the world in a single day, the financial system gained the power to condition countries and bring about abrupt collapses in the confidence in an economy. One such tool is through the derivatives market. Derivatives are a risk-assessment tool that is not regulated by the Securities and Exchange Commission (SEC), they are mainly traded over-the-counter (OTC) without publicizing the contract over exchanges. The mortgage-backed securities of Lehman Brothers were largely insured by Credit Default Swaps (CDS). The derivative market linked together investment banks, mortgage-backed securities and insurance companies, making the failure of one institution a systemic threat to the capitalist system. The value of the overall derivatives market is estimated by the Bank for International Settlement (BIS) to be around $83 trillion for the futures market, $594 trillion for over-the-counter exchanges, and central to the credit market $57 trillion in CDS in June of 2008.[1]

While these CDSs and derivatives do have some link to an underlying asset, albeit a far removed one, the growth in this market, particularly when firms leverage billions to hedge against risk using CDSs, is a modern account of what Marx called fictitious capital. As Marx stated:

> All this paper actually represents nothing more than accumulated claims, or legal titles, to future production whose money or capital value represents either no capital at all, as in the case of state debts, or is regulated independently of the value of real capital which it represents ... In all countries based on capitalist production, there exists in this form an enormous quantity of so-called interest-bearing capital, or moneyed capital. And by accumulation of money-capital nothing more, in the main, is connoted than an accumulation of these claims on production, an accumulation of the market-price, the illusory capital-value of these claims.[2]

The nearly $600 trillion dollars is not invested in an underlying asset where actual commodities are produced. Rather this money is invested to mitigate the risk of an asset declining in value. Essentially, investment firms bet whether an asset will gain value and profit if it does. Hedge funds can also short sell an asset. Short selling occurs when investors bet a stock or asset will lose money then reap a profit if the value of a stock declines.[3] This financial tool was brought into markets as an incentive for investors to publicize bad business practices. However, since the market is largely unregulated, shorting a firm can set off a panic, turning a minor downturn into a crisis. Nothing tangible is produced despite the vast amounts of money. The role of derivatives was largely ignored until the collapse of the American housing market, turning a recession into a global economic crisis.

The downturn in the American housing market began in 2007 and led to a full financial crisis in the autumn of 2008. The long-term determinants of the crisis range from the American proclivity towards homeownership to the gradual loosening of regulations over finance and mortgage lending since the 1980s. A key institutional change passed by Congress in 1999, the Financial Services Modernization Act, eliminated the barrier between commercial and investment banks, leading to the securitization of mortgages—bundling together numerous mortgages for the purposes of investment. This Act also struck down one of the most significant regulations, the Glass-Steagall Act passed during the Great Depression, though many of the provisions of the Act have already been avoided by financial firms. The liberalization of mortgage terms led homeowners to take out variable-rate interest mortgages in order to finance the purchases of a home; by 2004–05, nearly one-third of all homes purchased in the USA had an adjustable rate.[4] The popularity of these loans was due to the availability of cheap credit, the lack of regulation over the term of mortgages, the seemingly endless rise in the value of the housing market and the sales practices by mortgage companies.

After the dot-com bubble burst and the terrorist attacks in 2001, the American Federal Reserve decided to keep interest rates low in order to prevent a recession. This was to resolve one crisis through a spatial fix by providing a highly profitable market for investors through housing.[5] This method of "solving" the recession in 2001 had two consequences: it led banks and investment firms to over-leverage to maximize their profits, and it created an incentive for individuals to take out mortgages with the knowledge that they would be able to sell their home for a substantial profit. However, since profits were so high, it created an incentive for lenders, the government and homeowners to expand the housing market by lowering the requirements for a mortgage. Homeowners with poor credit were offered mortgages at variable or subprime interest rates—that was lending to people who were deemed medium to high risk. In 2002, subprime loans made up only 6% of overall mortgages; by 2007, nearly 30% of mortgages were subprime.[6] In order to finance these mortgages, banks securitized, or bundled together, mortgages into Collateralized Debt Obligations (CDOs) and sold them to investors. From 2002 to 2006, the general value of houses in the USA increased, allowing everyone involved in the mortgage market to make a substantial profit.[7] Beginning in 2006, an increasing amount of foreclosures led to a downturn in the value of the housing market, creating a cascade of problems for the overall economy.

Financial institutions could borrow vast sums of money to invest in mortgages due to arbitrage between the American and Chinese economies. China began to develop at an extremely rapid pace throughout the 1990s and early 2000s, largely due to its cheap labour and the low value of its currency.[8] From 1995 to 2005, US consumers borrowed at low interest rates and then some corporations and firms invested that money into the dot-com firms and the housing markets.[9] For consumers, this also kept interest rates low. The rest of the world relies upon US consumer demand in order to the buy goods produced in emerging economies. Consequently, countries such as China were willing to lend the Americans money in order to keep the process going. If this easy liquidity were to dry up, it would place pressure on Federal Reserve to raise interest rates to attract capital, but it would also make borrowing far more costly to Americans thereby slowing consumption. To prevent this from taking place, the Chinese kept purchasing US debt in order to fund American private and public spending.[10] This is an obvious contradiction in the relationship between China and America. China is America's largest modern geopolitical competitor, but it is also the country that is financing its consumer debt and military spending. Despite the unity of global economy, there may be tension and conflict on the political level. The financial markets push the two countries together, but political leaders are hesitant about a closer partnership.

The system of arbitrage was disrupted when the decline in the housing market took place in 2007 and began to have significant repercussions on the American and global economy. The problem started with the investment firms Bear Stearns, which required a bailout in the spring of 2008 and was eventually sold to JP Morgan. The downturn of the financial industry became even more evident when two government-backed institutions, Fannie Mae and Freddie Mac, which invested heavily in subprime loans, required government intervention in September 2008. By the end of 2008, the problem became cyclical: many homeowners who took out subprime loans had their interest rates rise, which led to greater difficulty refinancing and selling their homes, placing further downward pressure on the housing market. Those capable of making their mortgage payments were left with negative equity—the value of their homes was less than the mortgage, leading to a substantial loss of savings. As foreclosures increased, banks were left with homes that could not be sold and were steadily decreasing in value. Furthermore, many major financial institutions were over-leveraged in order to sell mortgages, making them even more vulnerable to a decline in the housing market. To make matters worse, investors, often afraid of losing money in an already fragile economic climate, were far less likely to invest in banks and institutions that had sold subprime mortgages, making liquidity increasingly scarce. These three factors led to what may have started as a downtown in the American economy becoming a global financial crisis.

Although the underlying problems in the housing market may have laid the foundations for a downturn in the US economy, the initiating factor for the crisis was the bankruptcy of the investment firm Lehman Brothers. Like many other firms, Lehman Brothers invested heavily in mortgage-backed securities. By September 2008, Lehman Brothers had $600 billion dollars worth of subprime mortgages.[11] These "toxic assets" led to a decline in stock value, and the inability to secure private-sector loans due to over-leveraging—it became increasingly evident Lehman would need a bailout like Bear Stearns and Fannie Mae and Freddie Mac. The US government made a key decision that had repercussions for the entire global economy—Treasury and the US Federal Reserve decided to break the precedent of bailing out institutions and let Lehman Brothers declare bankruptcy. This was a surprising outcome given the history of Washington and Wall Street. The financial industry has had open access to US policy-makers and the Federal Reserve, often dictating the terms of the regulatory debate.[12] Wall Street firms have a vast pool of lobbyists both outside and within government, with many members of the Treasury Department coming directly from the financial sector.[13]

So when the Federal Reserve and Treasury did not provide a loan to Lehman Brothers, it had dramatic effects on the global economy.

The immediate reactions of both domestic and international markets were severe: credit markets froze as the market for commercial paper dried up.[14] Banks could no longer risk lending to each other. The crisis went global and by the end of October most major stock markets were down by around 30%.[15] According to the International Labour Organization, by the end of 2009, 34 million people across the global had lost their jobs due to the recession that followed the crisis (a statistic which does not include those underemployed or already unemployed).[16] The decline in the US housing market after the bankruptcy of Lehman Brothers spread to other countries: AIG, a global insurance company almost went bankrupt due to insuring mortgages with CDSs; Britain's Northern Rock was nationalized; and Iceland had a banking crisis. These events led Britain's *The Economist* to argue that "the world economy is "entering a major downturn" in the face of "the most dangerous shock" to rich-country financial markets since the 1930s".[17]

The crisis that resulted from the Lehman Brothers bankruptcy initiated a financial panic throughout the global economy. The housing market went through a period of boom—where investors and banking institutions amassed vast profits—which was followed by panic requiring government intervention. Where this crisis differed is that it was started in the largest economy in the world and the government acted atypically by not providing public money for a bailout.[18] The resulting collapse of Lehman Brothers threatened the stability of the entire global financial system. The USA deregulated its financial markets from the 1970s onwards in order to strengthen its economy against competitors, but the credit crunch had the opposite outcome. By 2008, New York had become central to the global financial system, with the Federal Reserve, Treasury and presidential administrations often capitulating to the demands of the financial industry (Panitch and Konings 2009). However, the very process that was intended to empower the USA undermined its economic stability and prosperity.

Furthermore, the financial crisis highlights the duality of the financial system. It is a transnational process of accumulation that can go where markets are open, but it takes on specific characteristics of the culture, institutions and politics of a country. Investment money can come from almost anywhere in the world. Yet financial markets have their own unique qualities which condition the response of governments to a crisis.

For example, since it was the global reserve currency, the USA has many methods at its disposal to mitigate the crisis, such as the TARP program and quantitative easing, that might otherwise be unavailable to another country.[19] The crisis showed the ability to spread a financial contagion from the USA to the rest of the world. Countries attached to the Euro cannot devalue their currencies and are constrained by their institutional commitments.[20] As the wide array of responses to the crisis showed, the recession is an uneven process that varies depending on the context, the level of financialization and the specific economic and political structure of a country.

THE CREDIT CRUNCH AND THE RESPONSE OF THE US GOVERNMENT

The credit crunch that followed the bankruptcy of Lehman Brothers led a crisis in the global financial system and a massive recession—a problem that persisted several years after the initial panic. Since the 1970s, America has been the main beneficiary of the financialization of the global economic system. In the past, Washington used its economic and political resources to prevent a financial panic from turning into a global catastrophe. There were numerous times throughout the 1980s and 1990s Washington intervened to prevent the failure of a major investment bank or a country defaulting on its loans. But by the turn of the millennium, finance capital had become too large for the American government to try to manage. When the American government allowed Lehman Brothers to declare bankruptcy, it sent a wave of panic throughout the global financial system. Investors were worried that even the largest firms could potentially fail and quickly withdrew from the financial system. The crisis may have started in the USA, but due to economic globalization, it quickly spread to Europe, South America and Southeast Asia.

After the collapse of Lehman Brothers, there was pressure on the US government to offer a bailout to the financial industry to unfreeze capital markets—the failure of AIG, JP Morgan and Bank of America would have dire repercussions for the global economy. However, contrary to the expectations of the financial industry, the initial stimulus bill—TARP—failed in the US House of Representatives, bringing markets to the point of collapse.[21] For political reasons, the US government would not ensure the viability of some of the most powerful banks in the financial system. Political leaders in one of the most powerful states that perpetuate Empire ignored the pressure of the financial system. Some of the largest financial corporations relied upon the Washington for a bailout to prevent their collapse. The US government acted contrary to the goals of finance capital, showing tension between politicians and the financial industry within the USA.

Initially, there was a consensus among wealthy industrialized countries to work together to mitigate the crisis. The G20 meetings in London and Pittsburgh were hailed as a success, with the hope of forging a "Bretton Woods II"—a new major regulatory regime of global finance.[22] Yet this accord quickly fell apart: there has been disagreement over the implementation of new financial regulations. Several key proposed policy changes have met with criticism from the international community. There are disputes over whether to implement new regulations, such as a proposed $2 trillion bank tax to pay for future bailouts, with Japan, China and Canada in opposition, with support from USA, UK and the rest of Europe.[23] While these conflicts may seem minor on the surface, each country is asserting its national interest based on the degree it has been affected by the financial crisis, not on the whims of the USA or the demands of the financial system.

American and British banks were over-leveraged and overexposed, requiring substantial government funds to bailout; the USA and UK would then benefit from a proposed bank tax. Canada and China did not require a massive bailout of their banking sectors, and a tax would penalize their intuitions despite their solvency during the crisis. Instituting new international regulations relies on countries independently agreeing to implement substantive policy changes. In the post-World War II period, America would act as the hegemon and others would tend to follow. Now, there appears to be little the Americans can do to compel other countries to enact new regulations.

Despite the problems of the crisis, the American financial system has the unique ability to attract capital due to its central position in the global economy. The USA serves as the global reserve currency, and its treasury bills are considered among the safest investments. This privileged position had led many critical theorists to assume the USA has control over the global financial system. Panitch and Gindin argue the increased intervention of the USA in the economy—particularly in the creation of too-big-to-fail corporations—expanded the USA's control over the international economy.[24] The US government willingly instituted the neoliberal policies that facilitated the creation and enlargement of the financial industry—the US Federal Reserve and Treasury were capable of bailing out intermittent crises.[25] Furthermore, the US government chose not regulate many of the financial tools used by the financial sector that led to the crisis. The repeal of the Glass-Steagall Act allowed deposit banks to engage in investment banking. Low interest rates were set and prolonged by the Federal Reserve, promoting over-leveraging and taking on riskier assets. The government also gave Fannie Mae and Freddie Mac explicit targets for lending to lower income people on subprime terms.[26]

The US government did institute many of the policies that led to the creation of financial crisis, however, the government could not control nor predict many of the consequences of these policies. Panitch and Gindin conflate the centrality of the USA in the international economic system, which is indisputable, with its control over the economic system. The American economy does give the government certain capabilities over its competitors, but the government does not automatically act in accordance with the wishes of finance capital. If this were the case, the US government would have bailed out Lehman Brothers or passed the first TARP bailout. Not doing so led to a loss of trillions of dollars in future bailouts and an increase in unemployment throughout America. Washington had already set a precedent to markets that the Federal Reserve was willing to bail out corporations, creating an expectation the government would act as lender of last resort. There was pressure on the US government to bail out Lehman Brothers, but was ignored by Congress. The best account behind letting Lehman Brothers fail was to reintroduce "moral hazard" to the banking system.[27] While the principle of moral hazard is an important ideal for capitalism, the US government had a history of not following this principle by previously bailing out Bear Sterns and Fannie Mae and Freddie Mac. It was willing to intervene when necessary to protect the interests of capital. However, because the US government did not know how much Lehman Brothers, or any other bank, held in mortgage-backed securities, nor the deep interconnection of the international financial system it led a crisis that threatened the entire capitalist system. Despite its centrality, America is still vulnerable to crises.

A contributing factor to the crisis was the American government's lack of regulation of derivatives. The decline of the housing market created a systemic crisis in the financial system. When Lehman Brothers went bankrupt, the CDSs were activated. However, the major insurer, AIG, did not have the money to pay the massive amount for Lehman's default on its debt. These derivatives represent trillions of dollars of fictitious capital that have minimal oversight by the US government. The sheer scope of the money in risk mitigation in the financial system dwarfs the size of the American or for that matter the global economy.

If the US government is directing the global financial system, and working for its benefit, there is no reasonable explanation why it left this multi-trillion dollar market unregulated or acted so contrary to its demands to the extent that it almost destroyed the American economy. The US government had information about the possible detrimental effects of OTC derivatives and CDSs, and there was even internal pressure from Treasury in the 1990s under the Clinton administration to regulate the derivatives market.[28] In 2002, Warren Buffet, a financial speculator who made billions in the 1990s, called derivatives "financial weapons of mass destruction" due to the incentive for financial institutions to increase the amount of risk and over-leverage.[29] However, regulation of this market was rejected by the Federal Reserve as going against the basic ideals of the free market. Indeed, derivatives are a part of the system—trillions of dollars of private unregulated money that has the ability to destroy corporations and governments at an unprecedented pace.

Eventually, the economic downturn and the prospect of a prolonged global depression put enough pressure on the US government to act, but even that reaction shows a clear indication of tension between politicians and capitalists that continue with the Obama presidency. When passing TARP, both Democrats and Republicans faced pressure from constituents not to bail out the financial industry.[30] In fact, Congress did not pass the first bailout package in September of 2008 which exacerbated the crisis. If the government was working in the interests of capital, the US government would not have acted so contrary to their demands. However, there were other determinants at work. Politicians were afraid of the voter backlash in the 2008 election and ignored the pressure the financial industry was putting on the government to introduce legislation to unfreeze credit markets to ensure no other major industries would collapse. In the face of a massive recession in 2009, there was even a political battle to pass Obama's stimulus plan. But even then, it has been criticized by a wide variety of academics and journalists. The economist Paul Krugman argued Obama's stimulus package did not go "far enough" in order to get the US economy growing and that much more spending is required.[31]

The economic situation had abated by the end of 2008 but still remained unfavourable: unemployment reached 9%, and the American economy grew by only 0.25% in 2009.[32] Growth since then was sluggish until 2015. Despite this, further stimulus spending was politically difficult—there has been significant pressure both inside government and from Tea Party groups to tighten government spending. The political pressure to do so has made significant interventions to regulate the economy difficult: TARP failed initially and Obama's stimulus plan was influenced largely by the political concerns of a Democratic Congress rather than the needs of the economy.[33] Political and economic motivations are not always harmonious. Politicians may act in order to promote the interests of capital, but due to their geographical and institutional position, political concerns often take priority over the demands of finance capital.

In times of economic crisis, the US government and the interests of the financial system can diverge. Policy outcomes to crises tend to be a catch-all shaped by domestic political considerations, ideology, and, only at times the needs of the economy. Also, the American government does not exclusively control its own nor the international economy. Although its wealth and central market position give it certain unique characteristics, there are aspects of the international economy, like derivatives and CDSs, that the SEC does not regulate. This makes it difficult to argue the government is directing global financial flows when they cause an economic meltdown in the USA. Though the US government does often work harmoniously with the interests of the financial industry, tensions can arise between these institutions when political motives and the needs of the financial sector diverge during times of crisis.[34] Two seemingly contradictory outcomes of this crisis have been to place further pressure on the US government to cater the interests of finance capital on the one hand and to create more conflict between politicians, the financial industry and the American public on the other. TARP and the Obama stimulus package gave the financial industry billions of dollars of public money in bailouts and tax breaks, while provoking small-government conservatives and libertarians in the USA. This is a clear tension between the demands of the capitalist system and the domestic considerations that come from the American public.

While it is the subprime mortgage crisis led to one of the largest contractions in the American economy since the Great Depression, it has not hampered the viability of America's economy, nor threatened its economic hegemony. As Eric Helleiner argues, the response to the Great Recession has empowered conservative movements and reinforced the economic primacy of the USA. Even following the devastating losses of 2008, American GDP growth had recovered by the middle of 2009, and actually grew at rate of 3.1% in the last quarter of 2010.[35] Although economic growth did slow to 1.9% in the first quarter of 2011,[36] which is not high by contemporary standards, this is still impressive given size of the US economy and the uncertainty present throughout the rest of the global economy. It is important to keep in mind that America is recovering from the worst financial crisis in 70 years, and four quarters of lost growth are actually a modest impact on the American economy as a whole. At the same time, the housing market—the catalyst of the recession—has stabilized over the past 3 years, with homes in most markets regaining the value they held in 2002, before the excesses of the subprime market.[37] Although readjustment represents a great deal of lost equity for homeowners and mortgage firms, the period from 2003 to 2007 was the exception for the housing market rather than the rule, in the sense that home prices were over-inflated due to low interest rates, cheap credit and low standards for borrowing. Yet even with the dramatic collapse of the housing market, by 2011 prices and home sales had stabilized at pre-bubble levels, and America had begun to experience modest levels of economic growth.

While it is difficult to assess whether the crisis is the harbinger of the end of American economic primacy, the impact of these crises should not be overstated. Even with the uncertainty surrounding its recovery from the Great Recession, America still accounts for roughly one-fifth of global economic output in 2009,[38] more than three times the total of any other state. Furthermore, compared to other countries, the American recession was neither as deep nor as prolonged as it otherwise might have been—a testament to the strength of the economy of the USA. Despite mounting concerns over its overall debt level, the American dollar still functions as the world's reserve currency, easily outstripping the Euro and the Yen as the medium in which international monetary transactions are denominated. As a consequence, while it cannot be denied that there are problems facing the American economy, it would be premature to suggest that due to the crisis alone America lost its position as the largest and most affluent actor in the global system or that these challenges will lead to the terminal decline in American economic primacy.

THE AMERICAN DEBT CEILING AND AN ARTIFICIAL CRISIS

Although by most accounts the USA is in a favourable position vis-à-vis the rest of the major countries in the global economy, its position as a central network in the capitalist system could be threatened by its domestic politics conflicting with the demands of the financial system, not due to the level of debt, or market forces undermining the American economic system. While crisis can be viewed as a positive for capitalists, often it forces open new markets or to privatize assets, a default on debt would undermine the entire capitalist system and threaten the assets of the wealthy. One such event took place in the summer of 2011 when the American government reached its debt ceiling. A political crisis ensued between President Obama who wanted to raise the limit while implementing tax increases on the wealthiest to lower the deficit and House Republicans who refused to agree to higher taxes and demanded substantial cuts to the budget.[39] The debt ceiling originated during the First World War to prevent the US government from deficit spending without the consent of Congress by establishing an arbitrary limit. The Republicans were using a default on American debt as a political tool to extract concessions from the Obama administration. The crisis lasted until the day of a potential default, with Obama agreeing with Republicans to cut $2.4 trillion from the budget for the debt ceiling to be raised past the 2012 presidential election.[40] While a crisis was averted, the polarization of the debate on such an important issue as America's debt does not bode well for the future of the USA within the capitalist system. For one, the spending cuts demanded by the Republicans are reminiscent of the cuts demanded by Congress during Roosevelt's presidency in 1938. Unemployment remains high in the USA as the TARP money did not translate into loans to consumers—most American financial institutions paid down debt or simply purchased US debt for a safe return.[41] Without banks lending to consumers, and the government initiating a series of austerity measures, there are fears the USA could fall, yet again, into crisis.

However, a more substantial matter is that the US debt ceiling was used for partisan politics with Republicans willing to allow the American government to go into default. Many Republicans in the House of Representatives were elected in 2010 advocating the libertarian views of the Tea Party which sought to dramatically reduce the intervention of government in the economy. A default was viewed by this group as a method to heavily constrain the Federal government—the USA would no longer be able to run a deficit.[42] The US Treasury would take "extraordinary measures" in order to pay down the minimum interest on the debt, but there would be massive cuts to social spending such as Medicare, Social Security and military personnel paychecks.[43] On the domestic front, the withdrawal of nearly 70% of government discretionary spending from the economy would grind consumer spending to a halt, leading to a massive recession.[44] This of course does not take into account the international ramifications of a default on US debt. The outcome for the global economy would be catastrophic. First, the collapse in American consumer demand would lead to a drop in trade for almost every economy that sells goods and services to the USA, which would affect almost every country in some form. Second, US Treasury bills denominated in US dollars—the world's reserve currency—would effectively be worthless, meaning that any country, government, corporation or pension fund that holds US debt would lose trillions.[45] Third, Treasury bills are also viewed as a baseline for other stocks and bonds due to the fact investors view US debt as the safest. Without such a barometer, financial markets would descend into chaos as investors would dump Treasury bills onto the market. The combined result of these three factors—plus numerous other unforeseeable negative outcomes—would have likely have led to the most protracted and dire global depression since the 1930s.[46]

With the severity of these consequences, it is surprising how quickly the Republicans proposed it as a way to curtail government spending, and how close the government came to defaulting on its debt. Previous increases to the debt ceiling have been relatively apolitical affairs: regardless of the administration, the debate is typically over budgetary matters rather than the total accrued debt. From its inception during the First World War, each time the debt limit was reached, Congress would often debate the issue and the US budget.[47] It was not politicized until

1995 when the Republicans under Newt Gingrich were in control of the House, but even in that case, the Republicans decided to target the budget rather than the debt ceiling. The politicization during the Obama administration over an issue of vital importance to the American and global economy is problematic for the long-term viability of the USA as a central network in capitalism. If another major crisis occurs—perhaps an investment bank failure or the potential default of a European economy—Washington may not respond, or enact policies that will exacerbate a crisis. The result could irreparably damage the global economy and undermine the USA as a global superpower.

Yet even with these stark consequences, there have been two other subsequent occasions when the US nearly defaulted on its debt. The second time was in the autumn of 2013 when Republicans refused to pass and threatened to, yet again, default on US debt by not increasing the debt ceiling due to the institution of the Patient Protection and Affordable Care Act. The sequester alone was damaging to the US economy causing almost 7,00,000 job losses and an almost 0.6% decline in GDP for the brief period of government shutdown.[48] Eventually, though within hours of the debt ceiling deadline, an agreement was reached between Republicans and Democrats to avert an economic disaster by increasing the debt ceiling and reopen government. The next time the debt ceiling limit was reached, in early 2014, it was increased without much political infighting in Washington, yet beneath, there remain tension between the Democrats and Republicans over the role of its national debt.

Each time the debt ceiling is temporarily lifted, often only for a few months, it requires a cross-section of Democrats and Republicans in Congress. Members of the House of Representatives come from smaller districts and represent a smaller constituency than Senators. Indeed, the votes in the House to increase the debt ceiling show an incredibly problematic trajectory. In the immediate aftermath of the election of Tea Party members in the 2010 midterms, the House eventually increased the debt ceiling on 1 August 2011, by a vote of 269–161; 174 Republicans and 95 Democrats voted for it, while 66 Republicans and 95 Democrats voted against it. In 2013, the House approved the measure 285–144. With 87 Republicans joined a united Democratic caucus, allowing Congress to meet a critical Treasury Department deadline with one day to spare.[49] In 2014, the numbers were even more striking with 221–201, which relied almost entirely on Democrats in the

Republican-controlled House to carry the measure. Only 28 Republicans voted yes, and only two Democrats voted no.[50] Each time the debt ceiling requires an increase, fewer Republicans vote in favour of doing so. While it would be premature to predict that an economic catastrophe is inevitable, as I will discuss in the next section, domestic political and financing laws substantially raise the prospect of a default in the near future.

If much of the research on the default on America's sovereign debt remains speculative, it is because its consequences would be so dire for both the US and global economy. It is incredibly difficult for many policy analysts to predict how far the economic chaos would spread. There would almost certainly be a global depression as markets panic in the wake of existing US treasuries essentially becoming worthless in a matter of days. China would be affected as its assets declined in value and much of its savings evaporated, and pension funds would lose a large portion of their value. Every person, institution and country that held US debt or US dollars would be immediately impacted by a default on US debt. The longer-term prospects also remain uncertain: there simply is, as of yet, no alternative widely accepted asset that could replace US debt in the global economy. Perhaps one, or a number, could develop after a protracted period of time. Moreover, this does not even address the political upheaval that would follow a massive global depression. One only needs to look at the rise in extremism in Europe due to the Euro crisis to envision a rise in political conflict. Indeed, even a temporary period of failing to raise the debt ceiling could lead to a global depression the world has not experienced since the 1930s.

POLARIZATION AND THE POLITICS OF DEFAULT

Prior to 2011, increasing the debt ceiling was a relatively apolitical affair. There was a brief period after the 1994 election when Newt Gingrich considered using the debt ceiling to extract concession from the Clinton Administration, but this was quickly abandoned to focus on the US budget. With the midterm elections of 2010 bringing in members of the Tea Party—a loosely affiliated group dedicated to small government and low taxes—as part of the Republican caucus, the debt ceiling became politicized, and the US government came within days of a default in the summer of 2011. There are three interrelated reasons to explain why this contradiction has come to the debt ceiling. The first reason is due to high incumbency rates in the US congressional districts. Most members of the House of Representatives have a significant advantage during elections and are in demographically "safe" districts with little competition from the opposing party. Along with this is the US primary system, which removes power from party elites and gives it directly to party members in the district. Thus, counter-intuitively, a member of the House often has more to fear from a primary challenger than from the opposing party in an election. Finally, the liberalization of campaign finance laws has freed up money to fund challengers to moderates in both parties. The very laws that allow for the wealthy to have more influence in American politics may ultimately undermine the entire economic system due to polarization. In culmination, this has led to a more polarized Congress, and one that is willing to politicize an issue as consequential as the debt ceiling.

Conflict extension partially explains why the debt ceiling has become politicized by party elites in the USA. Certain issues in the USA, such as welfare, gun rights and abortion, have become polarized along party lines.[51] The reason for this polarization is simple: there is no firm consensus on these issues in American society. There is a sizable portion of the population that believes in one policy, and another portion that holds a contrarian perspective. Thus, the political parties merely reflect the views of their constituents. Parties adopt either conservative or liberal policies to attract certain segments of the electorate. Despite the dire consequences, defaulting on US debt has a base of support in the electorate. In a CNN poll around the 2013 debt ceiling and sequester crisis, 56% of Americans said it would be a bad thing if it was not raised, with 38% saying it would be a good thing for the country.[52] While 38% is not a majority, it is a large enough segment of the population to support the obstructionism in Congress. Political parties are aligning along a conservative/liberal spectrum in regards to the debt ceiling to attract votes and as a reflection of the views of their constituents.

These partisan views are further exaggerated by the composition of Congressional districts and the advantages of incumbency. In the latter part of twentieth and early twenty-first centuries, nearly 95% of incumbents on average were re-elected to their positions in Congress—this is partially due to gerrymandering, fundraising advantages and name recognition.[53] Unlike many other countries which rely on an independent national body to form electoral boundaries, Congressional districts are decided by state governments and are highly politicized. Both parties, in fact, have an interest in protecting incumbents in an election, and thus Congressional districts are shaped to exaggerate this advantage.[54] Moreover, incumbent has the financial resources to outspend their competitors. On average, House incumbents, regardless of political affiliation, outspent their rivals $1.7 million to $5,87,000, a ratio of almost a 3–1. Incumbent senators spent on average $10.7 million compared to $7.2 million for challengers.[55] This is a considerable hurdle for challengers to overcome in order to run for office. For the debt ceiling, the incumbency re-election rate insulates members of Congress from electoral consequences of poor policy decisions, if, in fact, members of their districts opposed raising the debt ceiling in the first place.

Another explanation for the large amount of members of Congress who refused to raise the debt ceiling is due to the presence of primaries. Elites within parties only have modest control over members of their own party that are nominated for Congress. Indeed, the basis of power for each member of Congress is not within the political party, but rather from their home districts. Ironically, the largest threat to a Congressperson is not from being defeated in an election, but rather from loses the party's primary to a far more ideologically "pure" candidate, since primaries are largely decided by Republican and Democratic activists. Particularly in the 2010 midterms, Tea Party members won against traditional Republican establishment candidates in 5 Senate races and 39 House races.[56] More importantly, though for policy decisions, the threat of primaries tends to force incumbents to their ideological extremes to ward off possible challengers.[57] In effect, political radicals do not need to get elected. Merely, the threat of a primary challenge is enough to force well-established candidates to adopt an obstructionist position on important issues like the debt ceiling. This could also potentially explain the far-reaching impact of the Tea Party beyond the relatively few candidates that are part of its official caucus. This, of course, makes building a consensus across party lines increasingly difficult, if even the relative power of the Tea Party wanes in the coming years. Primaries then serve to further polarize Congress, making consensus on major issues where the parties differ on policy much more difficult.

Finally, money and relaxed campaign finance laws play a role in the polarization of the US Congress. Running for Congress is extremely expensive: the average House race costs nearly $2 million, while Senators have to raise almost $10 million to run for office.[58] Yet this is relatively small compared to the amount of money spent by private donors to influence the electorate. In 2010, the Supreme Court struck down existing campaign finance laws in the *Citizens United versus FEC,* lifting the already weak limit on corporations, individuals or unions spending money to elect or defeat a candidate. In the 2012 election cycle alone, Political Action Committees or PACs spent over $567 million on presidential and congressional races.[59] The US electoral system is flooded with money, which along with a politicized news media, amplifies the policy differences between the two political parties.[60] This creates a feedback loop between politicians, PACs, and the media: politicians have an incentive to take an extreme position on an issue, PACs will either provide money to support or oppose this position, and this view is promulgated by news broadcasters.[61] In fact, politicians are aware of this feedback loop and use simple ideological messages that it can be repeated through the media and in political ads.[62] The incentives then are for candidates to follow the party's position, obstruct any policies of their opponent and use the media and money from PACs to ensure their re-election. For moderate candidates that seek consensus away from the party line, there is also a readily accessible pool of money to be spent on their defeat. The Citizens United decision did not create this system—private money already had a presence in American elections—it merely removed another barrier between moneyed interests and the political class.

In sum, each of these factors provides some insight into why Congress experiences a crisis each time the USA reaches its debt limit. Members of Congress, particularly in the House of Representatives, align themselves around wedge issues. From there, there is a high degree of incumbency due to a combination of money, name recognition and gerrymandering. Finally, there is a nexus between politics, easily accessible money, and the news media that further exacerbates the polarization between Republicans and Democrats. Members of each party have both an electoral and economic incentive not to reach a consensus with the opposition. If a candidate does deviate from the party line, there is both the money and a primary process to force a candidate to reconsider their position. This is one of the reasons why Congresses elected since 2010 have been so unproductive—the 110th Congress, elected in the wake of the 2010 midterms—passed only 173 laws—far fewer than the infamous "do-nothing" Congress during Truman's tenure of 1947–48.[63] While each party has an incentive in continuing this gridlock, the tone this has sent to the American public—political inaction in the face of crisis—has the potential to ultimately jeopardize America's position as the global hegemon or lead to a mounting frustration with the system from the citizens to create a political backlash.

American Hegemony After the Recession

Despite the tumultuous domestic situation, the USA has actually faired rather well in the long-term aftermath of the Great Recession. While financial markets may have reacted poorly to policy decisions and inaction from the US government, eventually the economy improved, real wages starting to rise and unemployment reached pre-crisis levels. Internationally, rather than a great restructuring of world order with power moving to the European Union or to China, the USA retained its economic and political hegemony. Indeed, many of the structural advantages of the USA: the role of the dollar as reserve currency, its dominance in international institutions and the ubiquity of US debt and centrality of its market have reinforced rather than undermine American hegemony. By 2016, the economic recovery was well underway: the American unemployment rate dipped below 5% of the labour force and real wages, which had stagnated, began to grow due to the increased demand for labour (Schwartz 2016). The Great Recession, then, proved to be a protracted economic downturn for the USA, but due to demographics, a stable country and its long-term role as global hegemon, from a systemic perspective, it looks as though American will remain the dominant country in international politics. Indeed, Eric Helleiner (2014) called the recession the "Status-Quo Crisis" where America retained its intuitional dominance on the international stage, however, as I shall continue to argue later, America's most significant threat is not from objective systemic factors or international threats, but from domestic pathologies that may jeopardize its hegemony.

Unlike previous periods discussed earlier, America's role in global affairs and international institutions did not decline in the wake of the Great Recession, indeed in the years following the crisis the USA remains a dominant actor. Even many of the key features of the pre-recession era remain or have been strengthened by the crisis, such as the neoliberal agenda of open markets and free trade, at least until 2016 (Helleiner 2014). In the aftermath of the Great Recession, as discussed earlier, there was a brief movement to regulate the financial system, but rather than substantive reforms being introduced, similar to the Bretton Woods era, most of the banking reforms were market-oriented, such as reserve requirements and "stress tests" were intended to preserve the integrity of the capitalist system. Most of the features of the pre-crisis system remain in place as well: international financial transactions move across borders without a "Tobin Tax", capital controls were not put in place, and monitoring OTC derivatives remain largely unchanged (Helleiner 2014). Part of the explanation for the lack of changes to the system has to do with role of US policy-makers. After the initial shock of the crisis, and certainly after 2010 midterm election, there remained little political will for the Americans to institute domestic and international reforms. The Americans remained committed to market-friendly approaches rather than introducing a series of anti-market reforms that would have constrained private financial interests. The other reason is a lack of pressure from other major partners in the G20—there was no broader international consensus on reforms. There were few new international institutions formed in the wake of the crisis and no new international financial architecture for the system. Neoliberal American-dominated orthodoxy won the day.

Despite the protracted long-term recession, America was capable of further entrenching the dollar, as central to the financial system. In response to the Great Recession, with the political situation in the USA making fiscal stimulus impossible after 2010, the Federal Reserve undertook three rounds of Quantitative Easing, adding more than 3.5 trillion to its balance sheet (Prasad 2014). The goal of this was to aid in the economic recovery of the USA by lowering interest rates and providing access to liquidity for financial institutions to incentivize borrowing money. Indeed, the Fed Reserve amplified the same policies that led to the recession in the first place: it made borrowing easier for the very institutions that over-leveraged. Traditionally, the scope of this liquidity would send a message to international institutions and corporations that the USA was in an economically precarious situation. Paradoxically through, these policies, along with the centrality and ubiquity of American dollars in the economy have actually strengthened American hegemony:

> The US economy is now too big and too important to stumble without pulling the rest of world down with it. If it were to experience a fiscal or financial meltdown, the reverberations would be damaging for every country in the world. Just the fear of this devastation points to how central the

US economy is to the global financial system. The dubious promise of safety from this very devastation is the irresistible lure of the dollar trap. The situation is rife with paradox. (Prasad 299: 2014)

Here we have an incentive problem, as has been discussed earlier in the chapter on China, for countries that may be opposed to US interests. The US dollar has become entrenched in the international financial system and has become an unavoidable method for financial transactions. Of course, this also makes other countries vulnerable to the policies of the Federal Reserve and the American government. Each time the Fed lowers interest rates and increases the money supply, it lessens the overall value of the dollar, yet other countries are too invested in the American financial system to find an alternative. The prosperity and stability of the international financial system are interlinked with the American economy. Hence if the USA experiences an economic downturn, as it did during the Great Recession, the contagion spreads throughout the rest of the financial system.

Despite the severity of the crisis, the recession did not change the overall neoliberal orthodoxy of US economic policy, at least in the medium term. Indeed, the solutions presented by the Obama administration, even in the early phase with Democratic majorities in the House and Senate between 2009 and 2011, were favourable to the banking industry. The largest investment banks not only received bailouts under the TARP system, but due to phases of Quantitative Easing could borrow money cheaply (Helleiner 2014). An explanation for the lack of alternatives to neoliberalism was due to the weakness of possible alternatives. While neoliberalism helped to facilitate an economic and political crisis in the Great Recession immediate alternatives were not readily available due to the lack of a counter-hegemonic project (Overbeek and van Apeldoorn 2012). While there were protests in Europe against austerity and an unfocused movement against the banks with Occupy Wall Street, these did not represent a significant challenge to neoliberal hegemony.

From a historical institutionalist perspective, the Great Recession was an unremarkable challenge to the dominance of the USA. The neoliberal market policies that had their origins in the late 1970s and early 1980s were not challenged, but merely subtle changes to the American and international finance system were put in place. Neoliberalism with its emphasis on open markets, trade, property rights and free exchange remained the dominant macroeconomic policy for the international system (Overbeek and van Apeldoorn 2014). The reforms that were put in place were friendly to the overall goals of the financial industry, requiring some oversight, but not qualitatively altering the pre-crisis institutional framework. The promise of a new Bretton Woods system with greater regulation and domestic control over finance quickly fell off the policy agenda. America remained a dominant player in international institutions, such as the IMF, G7 and G20. In the international financial system, the American dollar, rather than weakened by the USA at the hub of the crisis, was further strengthened as the reserve currency. Disparate countries, even those that supposedly are contenders for American hegemony such as China and Russia, have incentives to hold US dollars, even as the Federal Reserve debases the currency and American political infighting reaches new levels of partisanship. The problem with American hegemony, then, is not from an international or domestic threat. Purely examining America by most indicators such as economic growth, unemployment rates, stock market levels, the role of the dollar in the financial system, the USA seems to have maintained its hegemony in the system. However, the real threat to its place as hegemon lies in its polarized and malfunctioning political system.

Trumpism and the Undermining of American Hegemony

The political infighting over the past few years is often dismissed as merely part of business-as-usual in Washington. As discussed earlier, political polarization is commonplace in American society. These periodic crises with the debt ceiling, the government shutdown, led many Americans to believe that both parties were simply out of touch with Americans and many began looking for a political outsider to solve this inaction. These scope of events, particularly in the wake of the Great Recession that unevenly impacted middle-class and working-class Americans, provided support for the successful nomination and election of Donald Trump as president during the 2016 election. Trump and what he represents is not an anomaly in American politics, but a cause of pre-existing pathologies in society that ultimately overwhelmed the Washington political establishment and could jeopardize American hegemony. The Tea Party originated with many Americans angry as the perceived overreach by the Obama administration in the area of healthcare. The fighting and political logjam between Republicans and

Democrats in the 2010–2016 period even further exacerbated the belief both parties were "broken" and controlled by financial interests, rather than working to help the American people. Ironically, Trump's ascent with his message of American declinism could not contrast further with the evidence: by the November election, the American economy was fairing far better than its European and Chinese counterparts. Yet Trump's message resonated with a sizable plurality of the American population to win the presidential election. The success of Trump and his radical views towards free trade, open markets and international institutions represents one of the largest challenges to contemporary American hegemony.

It is not historically unprecedented for domestic politics to have large ramifications on international order and stability. Indeed, one of the cornerstone texts in International Relations theory recognizes the "second image" or the domestic politics of a country may be a driving force behind foreign policy (Waltz 1959). In America's case, the presidential campaign of Donald Trump, a New York developer and Reality TV star, was initially met with scorn, humour and derision, both from the political establishment and the media. He launched his campaign in Trump Tower, New York by calling Mexicans "rapists and drug dealers", promised to build a wall between the USA and Mexico, ban Muslims entering the USA as the campaign progressed. Initially, it was assumed that Trump's chances would fade as the early primaries and caucuses began and that Republicans would favour candidates more palatable to the mainstream. While Trump's antics garnered him considerable media attention, many pollsters predicted Trump's popularity would fade as more Republicans became interested in the race and voted in primaries (Silver 2015). However, they underestimated several important factors that differed in the 2016 cycle. Trump had touched upon a level of anti-establishment that was exacerbated by the inaction in Washington in response to the crisis, along with the racial resentment that went with the first African American president and broader demographic changes to American society (Tesler 2016). Trump promised that he was the solution to the gridlock in Washington and that his business acumen could bring about an economic renewal for Americans who were impacted by the recession and globalization. Trump was also the champion of the Birther movement, a racist attempt to "prove" President Obama was not an American. In tandem, Trump was able to form, and keep, a coalition of voters who were angry at the establishment throughout the primary process.

In the early primaries, Trump faced a divided field of mainstream Republicans, which led him to electoral success in the New Hampshire and South Carolina primary, despite losing the Iowa Caucus. Each of the "mainstream" establishment Republicans had significant problems attracting a large enough base of voters to challenge Trump's 30–35% support. Of the leading challengers, Jeb Bush had the most financial resources, but had a difficult time separating himself from the legacy of his unpopular brother, while Florida Senator Marco Rubio had poor debate performances and was considered weak on immigration. Throughout the primary processes, mainstream Republican voters did not have a clear frontrunner to support to oppose Trump, so they ended up dividing their votes among numerous other candidates, leading to a victory by Donald Trump in New Hampshire and in South Carolina. By the end of Super Tuesday in March, a date for numerous simultaneous primaries, despite his divisive rhetoric, Trump's early wins led him to be the frontrunner to win the Republican primary. There was a final attempt by the Republican establishment to prevent Trump from becoming the nominee, but the momentum was on Trump's side, by May, in an almost unprecedented event in modern American history, an outsider with no government or military experience gained enough delegates to be the Republican nominee for president.

Initially, the Trump presidential campaign seemed like a historical aberration for an established political party as the Republican Party. Trump eschewed Many of the long-standing traditions of American elections: consolidating the establishment of the party, trying to appeal to undecided and moderate voters, spending money on advertising and get-out-the-vote staff. His opponent, former Secretary of State, First Lady and Senator Hillary Clinton, appeared to have an overwhelming amount of support both in the popular vote and in the ever-important Electoral College. Moreover, Trump promised to substantially alter the international economic and security framework should he be elected. Several of these promises included renegotiating or fully withdrawing from NAFTA, undermining the NATO alliance, easing relations with Putin's Russia, providing nuclear armaments to Japan and South Korea and committing war crimes by bombing the families of supposed sympathizers of ISIS (Paletta 2016). While much of this can be interpreted as the campaign rhetoric of someone with little foreign policy experience, it does enter into the political discourse and send to message to allies and partners that the USA is no longer politically willing to act as global hegemon of the international order. Trump's popularity was partially due to him being an outsider from the Washington establishment—both the Republicans and the Democrats—and his willingness to challenge long-standing norms of American political discourse and policy. Similar to the unexpected outcome of the Brexit vote discussed earlier, Trump surprised many observers, pollsters, and pundits by winning the 2016 presidential election and becoming the 45th president of the USA.

While the institutional limitations of the presidency should not be ignored, there remains a great deal of agency in the presidency, particularly since the Republicans also hold majorities in Congress. Prior to the election, Tea Party Republicans' mistrust of government and the system moved Congress to almost default on the debt ceiling and shut down the government. Thus, Trump is a consequence of this anger and frustration with government rather than the exception. With a mandate to govern, his supporters will expect him to fulfil at least some of his campaign promises, and while Trump has alienated many Republicans in Congress, there will be an inevitable push to enact policy with their newfound control of the legislative and executive branches, some on Trump's terms. Furthermore, rather than an aberration, there have been numerous successes for Right-wing Populists in countries like Britain, the Philippines, Poland, Austria, Hungary, and France (Greven 2016). The election of Trump as the American president can only further spread scepticism of elites, the popularity of closing borders, nativism, xenophobia, and racial resentment. The success of Trump, and those sharing his ideas, sets a precedent for other countries, legitimizing this brand of politics and potentially undermining the liberal consensus that has been the cornerstone of the international system since the end of the Second World War. While one isolated case could be ignored, multiple countries falling to populists could make for a rejection of the current system and renewal of hypernationalism.

Due to structural limitations and the trappings of being the world's hegemon, there has been a great deal of foreign policy continuity from administration to administration. The American presidency is relatively weak in the realm of domestic policy, but has a greater degree of discretion over foreign policy. Whether Trump will continue to uphold America's role as global hegemon by providing assurances to Eastern Europe in the face of a Russian threat, or continue the Pacific Pivot against China remains uncertain. There has never been an American president in modern history like Trump, unwilling to accept the role of the USA as a status quo power and uphold the very institutions that have been the hallmark of American hegemony. An underlying assumption in the historical institutionalist literature is that the domestic politics of the USA will not undermine its own role in these institutions (Helleiner 2014; Prasad 2014). The election of Trump, along with a general dissatisfaction of the American public with elites, government and institutions, could place pressure on the governing Republicans to alter America's long-standing support for these institutions. Sensing this lack of commitment, markets could react in a way that could throw the global economy into another recession or further undermine the global economy recovery, thereby incensing even more populist sentiment against the system. The election of Donald Trump as president has introduced uncertainty about the role of the USA as hegemon.

Summary

The USA is an important network in the international capitalist system, but it too can face problems beyond its control due to the tension between its political interests and the demands of the economic system. While it is premature to argue that the financial crisis undermined America's dominant role in the global economy, it does indicate that there are significant tensions, and potential contradictions, between the American government and global finance in times of crisis, particularly in the wake of the 2016 presidential election. The deregulation of the American financial sector in the late 1990s coupled with low interest and high savings from China and South Asia led to an inflating housing market in many developed countries. When prices collapsed in 2008, forcing Lehman Brothers into bankruptcy, international financial markets expected the US government would act as lender-of-last resort. Domestic politics took priority over the bailout of Lehman Brothers as well as the initial TARP package leading to conflict between the financial system and the US government. These diverging interests led to the failure of Lehman Brothers, which froze credit markets, and the failure of the first TARP bailout further exacerbated the crisis.

It is undeniable America has been a central network for the capitalist system, often leading the way to opening new markets and liberalizing finance. Yet after the 2008 credit crunch, it too has been trying to manage a crisis in capitalism. America's centrality should not be conflated with the assumption it has control over the capitalist system. Certainly, its large wealthy consumer base and its status as the world's reserve currency provide it unique capabilities, but finance is global in scope and larger in wealth than the US real productive economy. The financial system compels countries to enact policies favourable to investors, financial firms, and corporations, yet the US government has reacted erratically to this pressure. This is due to domestic political pressure from Americans and the structure of the US political system. Providing public loans to the financial industry has proven unpopular for left-wing Democratic and right-wing Republicans. Also, the Tea Party Republicans have proven to be obstructionist when it comes to even simple functions of the government, such as raising the debt ceiling which up until 2011 was a standard procedure. Though America may have a relatively strong economy considering the depths of the recession, its politics have proven to be a barrier to its recovery from the Great Recession, and there are worrying signs with the 2016 presidential election of a candidate who has campaigned on overturning the global order its politics rather than economic factors could undermine its position as global hegemon.

Notes

1. Bank of International Settlements. "Amounts outstanding of over-the-counter (OTC) derivatives". *BIS Quarterly Review.* (June 2010): 121.
2. Karl Marx, *Capital Volume 3.* (International Publishers, NY: Marx.org 1996): 4. http://www.marxists.org/archive/marx/works/1894-c3/ch29.htm.
3. The Economist. "Getting to the naked truth". *The Economist.* (12 February 2012): http://www.economist.com/node/21547254.
4. John Bellamy Foster and Fred Magdoff. *The Great Financial Crisis* (New York; Monthly Review Press, 2009): 33.
5. David Harvey. *Limits to Capital* (London; New York: Verso, 1999): xvi.
6. John Waggoner. "Subprime woes could spill over into other sectors". *USA Today.* (15 March 2007): http://www.usatoday.com/money/perfi/columnist/waggon/2007-03-15-subprime-woes_N.htm.
7. Ibid.
8. Herman Schwartz "Housing, Global Finance, and American Hegemony: Building Conservative Politics One Brick at a Time". *Comparative European Politics.* Vol. 6. (2008): 263.
9. Ibid., 263.
10. Ibid., 264.

11. Sam Mamudi. "Lehman folds with record $613 billion debt". *Marketwatch.* (15 September 2008): http://articles.marketwatch.com/2008-09-15/news/30748651_1_lehman-bonds-debt-lehman-brothers-holdings.
12. Eric Helleiner and Stefano Pagliari "The End of Self Regulation?" *Global Finance in Crisis.* Eds. Eric Helliener, Stefano Pagliari, Hubert Zimmerman (Routledge: New York: 2010): 76.
13. Ibid.
14. Andrew Ross Sorkin, "Lehman Files for Bankruptcy; Merrill Is Sold". *The New York Times.* (14 September 2008): A1.
15. The Economist. "The World Economy: Bad, or Worse". *The Economist* (9 October 2008): http://www.economist.com/node/12381879.
16. The International Labour Organization. *Global Employment Trends, January 2010* (Geneva: February 2010): 9.
17. The Economist. "The World Economy: Bad, or Worse". *The Economist* (9 October 2008).
18. Graham Turner, *The Credit Crunch.* (London: Pluto Press, 2008): 136.
19. Ibid., 188.
20. Ibid., 53.
21. The Economist. "The TARP Trap". *The Economist.* (20 November 2008): http://www.economist.com/node/12651125.
22. George Parker and Tony Barber. "European call for 'Bretton Woods II'". *The Financial Times.* (16 October 2008): http://www.ft.com/cms/s/0/7cc16b54-9b19-11dd-a653-000077b07658.html#axzz27PTqOLha.
23. Alan Beattie and Tom Braithwaite. "Nations struggle to find consensus on bank taxes". *The Financial Times.* (24 April 2010): http://www.ft.com/intl/cms/s/0/cccaa0a0-4f38-11df-b8f4-00144feab49a.html#axzz27PTqOLha.
24. Leo Panitch and Sam Gindin *Global Capitalism and American Empire* (Peterborough: Fernwood Publishing Company, Limited Dec. 2003): 261.
25. Ibid., 261.
26. Russell Roberts. "How Government Stoked the Mania". *The Wall Street Journal.* (3 October 2008): A21.
27. The Economist. "The Price of Failure". *The Economist.* (2 October 2008): http://www.economist.com/node/12342689.
28. David Cho and Zachary A. Goldfarb. "U.S. Pushes Ahead With Derivatives Regulation". *The Washington Post.* (14 May 2009): http://www.washingtonpost.com/wp-dyn/content/article/2009/05/13/AR2009051302393.html.

29. Warren Buffett. "Berkshire Hathaway Inc: 2002 Annual Report". (2003):15.
30. John Gapper. "TARP Travels Down a Hazardous Road". *The Financial Times*. (8 December 2009): http://www.ft.com/intl/cms/s/0/afcd2b4a-e399-11de-9f4f-00144feab49a.html.
31. Paul Krugman. "The Obama Gap". *The New York Times*. (8 January 2009): A27.
32. United States Department of Labor. "Employment Situation Summary" United States Department of Labor. Washington D.C. (2010): http://www.bls.gov/news.release/empsit.nr0.htm
33. The Economist. "The Obama Rescue". *The Economist*. (12 February 2009). http://www.economist.com/node/13108724.
34. Paul Krugman, "Wall Street Whitewash". *The New York Times*. (17 December 2010): A39; Andrew Ross Sorkin. *Too Big to Fail: The Inside Story of How Wall Street and Washington Fought to Save the Financial System*. (USA; Pengiun Books, 2009).
35. US Department of Commerce, "US Economy at a Glance: Perspective from the BEA Accounts", *US Department of Commerce*. Washington, DC. (12 July 2011), http://www.bea.gov/newsreleases/glance.htm.
36. Ibid.
37. Maureen Maitland and David Blitzer, "S&P/Case-Shiller Home Price Indices 2010, A Year In Review". *S&P Indices; a Year in Review*, (January 2011), http://www.standardandpoors.com.
38. International Monetary Fund, "World Economic Outlook Database—October 2010: Nominal GDP list of countries", International Monetary Fund. (2010) http://www.imf.org/external/pubs/ft/weo/2010/02/weodata/index.aspx.
39. James Politi, "US retreats from brink of debt default". *The Financial Times*. (3 August 2011): http://www.ft.com/intl/cms/s/0/2e95a7ae-bd28-11e0-9d5d-00144feabdc0.html.
40. Ibid.
41. The Economist, "Contagion, What Contagion?" *The Economist* (3 December 2011): http://www.economist.com/node/21541020.
42. Charles Krauthammer, "Our Salutary Debt-Ceiling Scare". *National Review*. (3 June 2011): http://www.nationalreview.com/articles/268707/our-salutary-debt-ceiling-scare-charles-krauthammer#.
43. Mindy R. Levit, et al. "Reaching the Debt Limit: Background and Potential Effects on Government Operations". *Congressional Research Service*. Washington, D.C. (31 May 2012): 2.
44. Ibid.
45. Ian Tilley, "Bernanke Warns on Debt-Limit 'Chaos'". *The Wall Street Journal*. (1 March 2011): http://blogs.wsj.com/economics/2011/03/01/bernanke-warns-on-debt-limit-chaos/.

46. Ibid.
47. Linda W Kowalcky and Lance T. Leloup "Congress and the Politics of Statutory Debt Limitation". *Public Administration Review*, 53. 1 1993).
48. Angelo Young. "Cost of Sequestering". *International Business Times.* 20 February 2013. http://www.ibtimes.com/cost-sequestration-700000-jobs-may-be-lost-across-board-budget-cuts-through-2014-gdp-growth-may-slow.
49. Lori Montgomery and Rosalind S. Helderman. "Obama signs bill to raise debt limit, reopen government". *The Washington Post.* 16 October 2013: http://www.washingtonpost.com/politics/house-effort-to-end-fiscal-crisis-collapses-leaving-senate-to-forge-last-minute-solution/2013/10/16/1e8bb150-364d-11e3-be86-6aeaa439845b_story.html.
50. Jonathan Wiseman and Ashley Parker. "House Approves Higher Debt Limit Without Condition". *The New York Times.* 11 February 2014. http://www.nytimes.com/2014/02/12/us/politics/boehner-to-bring-debt-ceiling-to-vote-without-policy-attachments.html?_r=0.
51. Geoffrey C. Layman and Thomas M. Carsey "Party Polarization and 'Conflict Extension' in the American Electorate". *American Journal of Political Science*, Vol. 46, No. 4 (October 2002), 782.
52. Paul Steinhauser "CNN Poll: Majority says raise debt ceiling" CNN politics. 2 October 2013.http://www.cnn.com/2013/10/02/politics/cnn-poll-debt-ceiling/.
53. John N. Friedman and Richard T. Holden "The Rising Incumbent Reelection Rate: What's Gerrymandering Got to Do with It?" *The Journal of Politics*, Vol. 71, No. 2 (April 2009), pp. 593–611
54. Ibid.
55. Paul Steinhauser and Robert Yoon, "Cost to win congressional election skyrockets" CNN politics. July 11, 2013. http://www.cnn.com/2013/07/11/politics/congress-election-costs/.
56. *The New York Times.* "How the Tea Party Fared". 4 November 2010. http://www.nytimes.com/interactive/2010/11/04/us/politics/tea-party-results.html?ref=politics.
57. David W. Brady, Hahrie Han and Jeremy C. Pope. "Primary Elections and Candidate Ideology: Out of Step with the Primary Electorate?" *Legislative Studies Quarterly*, Vol. 32, No. 1 (February 2007): 80.
58. David Graham. "How Big Money Created the Most Polarized Congress in a Century". *The Atlantic.* 9 July 2013. http://www.theatlantic.com/politics/archive/2013/07/how-big-money-created-the-most-polarized-congress-in-a-century-5-charts/277611/.
59. Nicholas Confessore. "Total Cost of Election Could Be $6 Billion". *The New York Times.* 31 October 2012. http://thecaucus.blogs.nytimes.com/2012/10/31/total-cost-of-election-could-be-6-billion/.

60. Thomas Ferguson. *Legislators Never Bowl Alone: Big Money, Mass Media and the Polarization of Congress.* INET Conference paper. April 2011: 8.
61. Ibid., 9.
62. Ibid.
63. Jennifer Steinhouer "Congress Nearing End of Session Where Partisan Input Impeded Output". *The New York Times.* 18 September 2012: http://www.nytimes.com/2012/09/19/us/politics/congress-nears-end-of-least-productive-session.html.

CHAPTER 7

The Coming Global Crisis

The purpose of this book has been to reconsider American hegemony from its rise after the First World War to the current period after the Great Recession through to the election of Donald Trump as president. I have examined American hegemony in the contemporary period. I have placed most of the emphasis on the USA as the dominant capitalist country since the Second World War, though at times I have examined other regions such as Europe and East Asia and other financial and international institutions. This book provided an analysis that offers insight to both the mainstream and critical literature. This recognizes that a hegemonic state is a multifaceted, contradictory, and complex expansionary force that varies depending on time and place. Throughout this discussion, I have sought to examine the historical origins of American hegemony and how it has been transformed by the ideational, political, economic and technological changes in the twentieth and early twenty-first century.

My analysis started shortly after the First World War as a point of departure, which coincided with the decline of the UK as the dominant state in the capitalist system and the ascent of the USA. I have discussed how system emerged due the Bretton Woods to the crisis of the Great Depression, which then collapsed in the 1970s with the rise of neoliberalism. America remains important to the promotion and regulation of the system, but more recently it too has been conditioned by international financial markets. Capitalism is itself a general and a specific process. Particularly since the deregulation of finance in the 1980s, it compels states to compete against each other for scarce resources, but also must find some place to be part of an accumulation cycle. Although financial markets are global in their breadth and scope, they are by no means abstracted from the geographical location of an economy. When it does find a location inevitably it interrelates with a region's history, culture and politics.

There are several conclusions that can be drawn about American hegemony and global capitalism in the wake of the Great Recession. The distinguishing feature of the global economy since the crisis has been the sheer power of the financial system to weaken even the largest economies. Rather than the demands of global finance dictating the policies of the Americans and Europeans, it is remarkable how unresponsive governments have been to the recession. This is mainly due to institutional and cultural factors. With their commitment to the Euro, the Northern Europeans have found it difficult and unpopular to continue to finance the debt of Southern Europe. This uncertainty has only further worsened the situation and has made possible solutions much more difficult. For the USA, the crisis has been exacerbated through inaction and government infighting. Even though Washington has a well-established history of bowing to the demands of the financial system, it too is constrained by domestic political and institutional factors. The polarization of the American electorate, along with the divided powers of the federal government, has led to an inadequate response to the crisis and the recession. America has only avoided facing a debt crisis similar to the Europeans due to its legacy as the hegemon of the international financial system and the reliance of the rest of the global economy on the American consumer market.

For the financial system, which has been the central focus my analysis of the global capitalist system since the 1980s, resistance and reform are far more complicated. As discussed throughout this book there has been a blurring between corporations and financial institutions, with many companies that used to produce goods now relying on financing for profitability. Moreover, many corporations are no longer bound to a single state, but have global production networks, further limiting the regulatory capacity of states. In the twentieth century, the state has been a useful apparatus to spread capitalism and punish opposition to finance capital and corporations. In the post-WWII period states even played an important role in regulating finance and establishing a stable economic system with the USA as the central actor. While it is likely impossible to return to the period of embedded liberalism, international agreements can have a role in mitigating the power of global finance should there ever be the political will to do so. Here is where the USA can leverage its key position to regulate international finance, if it has the political will to do so. There was some discussion from major countries in the immediate post-2008 crisis to forge a new international economic system, but this consensus quickly dissolved. There are simply too many incentives and powerful interests for countries, particularly the major financial centres of the USA and the UK, not to enact meaningful regulation on financial markets. Individual corporations or financial institutions can be targeted and CEOs can, but more often do not, go to jail, but this ignores the fact that the problem is systemic.

Financial firms and corporations have had 40 years to amass power and political influence. The role unregulated finance plays in the modern global economy must start to be contested. One of the few positive outcomes of the financial crisis and the recession is that it has brought attention to the social costs of financialization. In the 1980s and 1990s, economic globalization was viewed as a positive and inevitable force that would bring prosperity to everyone. With the possible exception of a few sycophants in the financial industry, media, and in academia, hardly anyone believes this myth anymore. In Europe, finance has ruined most of the economies and governments are left trying to stop the haemorrhaging. There have been periodic bailouts with the hope that the crisis will abate. Europeans must now live with harsh austerity measures and reduced social spending. Even with these measures, there is a possibility the Eurozone will collapse due to the pressure of financial markets. In the USA, ironically both the Tea Party and the Occupy movements are angered by the nexus between finance and the government—albeit with a different emphasis on the culprit. Despite the rhetoric from Obama and Trump, the American government has been unable to meaningfully regulate international finance.

This does not, however, suggest that rethinking the role of finance capital is impossible; it requires political will, international consensus from major stakeholders, and people willing to risk producing tangible goods instead of finding easy profits through finance. The overall thesis of this book is that the greatest threat to global economic stability is due to the politics of the USA, but in a contradictory manner, it is simultaneously uniquely positioned to reform the system if it has the political will to do so. After the Great Depression and the Second World War, there was a broad-based agreement from countries, capital and labour to limit the potentially destructive power of finance. As unlikely as this appears in a modern context, particularly with the election of Donald Trump and the dominance of the Republican Party, but the architecture for some democratic oversights exists. New York and London are centres of global finance, and are thus amenable to regulation should there be new comprehensive laws introduced and enforced. Heads of governments were at one point after the crisis considering new guidelines for financial firms, including a bank tax, and greater government oversight over investment banks. However, before too long finance capital and domestic political and economic considerations took precedent over meaningful reform of the system. In an unfortunate turn of events, attention has shifted from the financial industry to sovereign debt to immigrants as the main economic problem in the global system.

Although the USA remains by most accounts the wealthiest dominant country in the world, its future in the system is by no means assured. The conflict between the demands of the financial system and incentives of politics may result in Washington ending its primacy through its own action or inaction. The misadventures in Afghanistan and Iraq have proved costly. Another expensive foreign policy campaign against potential "rogue states" like Iran or North Korea could bolster America's competitors into taking a more assertive response and further undermine the USA'S fragile economy. However, if the events of the past few years are an indication of what is to come, it may be the internal problems of the American political system that undermine it global position rather than overreach alone. The USA has a privileged position in the international financial system, but through its own actions, it may jeopardize its hegemony. For example, if the USA decided to allow major investment firms to collapse, the credit markets to freeze, or to default on its debt as it almost did in the summer of 2011, this may lead to irreparable damage to both the American and global economy. The cases of Southern Europe show the power of financial markets to undermine a country's economy. Although unlikely in the short-term, it is not unthinkable a conflict between capitalism and Washington could occur as it did in September 2008. With the election of Trump as president—a man who campaigned against the current global order—the prospect of America undermining its own hegemony has grown considerably.

For most of the twentieth century, the USA has been central to expansion of capitalism, but it is not essential to its continuance. As Britain was once a hegemonic power that was replaced by the USA, it is conceivable an alternative country could overtake America as the main state within capitalism. As discussed though, at this time, major contenders have a long way to go before they replace the USA. In the years since the crisis, especially with the decline of energy prices in 2015, other geopolitical contenders such as Russia have been economically weakened. However, if current pathologies continue, it is more plausible regional actors will eventually replace America in matters of economics. In Europe, Germany has taken a leadership role in dealing with the PIIGS sovereign debt crisis through the ECB and the EFSF. If it were just 10 years ago, the USA would almost certainly have played a more dominant role, as it did during the peso and East Asia crisis. The legacy of the Bush administration has left the American government with fewer economic resources and less political influence worldwide. Whether America's withdrawal from European affairs is due to its economic problems at home and not a protracted trend in global politics remains to be seen.

Regardless of the dominant country in the international system, a major systemic source of conflict in the twenty-first century will be capitalism. In recent years, financial markets have led to crisis in the American and European economies. And while China seems to have been left relatively unscathed from the recession, there are warning signs of problems, especially with its stock market and housing market. Few countries can isolate themselves from the international financial system. This is due to the breadth and scope of the modern capitalist. Critics often suggest that too-big-to-fail firms caused the financial crisis, but as I have shown, the dominance of financial firms and the protection of investors is, in fact, an effect of a multitude of historical processes. Though countries may create institutional barriers against rapid fluctuations, 40 years of liberalizing financial markets along with innovations in communication and transportation technology have fundamentally changed the global economy. People can potentially invest in any market anywhere in the world where it is profitable. In response, states have instituted policies to attract investment, effectively making finance a transnational phenomenon. The sheer size, breadth and complexity of the modern forms of fictitious capital defy the understanding and control of both governments and many in the financial industry. As experienced during the crisis of 2008, the collapse of one American investment firm nearly brought down the entire global economic system. Since then almost every major government has enacted policies to mitigate the effects of the recession with varying degrees of success.

If these forces of are indeed problematic, then a topic which mirrors this discussion is how reform is possible. Although thus far I have avoided a broad evaluation of this issue, these are some tentative suggestions. We must try to understand the process of capitalism at work and how they interact with the cultural, political and social context. These are not always easy to differentiate since an event often has multiple forces at work. But from there, a plan for resistance can be formulated. Foreign policy is often determined by the geopolitical distribution of power in the international system and by domestic factors. The fall of communism brought a new unipolar system with the USA as the lone superpower. It no longer had a competitive military power to prevent its foreign policy excesses. Under President Clinton, this led America to expand the role of markets throughout the global economy. When George W. Bush came to power, American foreign policy changed due to the terrorist attacks of 11 September 2001, with the principles of pre-emptive strike and democracy promotion through force.

Recent history suggests that this can be combated in two ways: by fostering international geopolitical opposition to the US government, or by domestic pressure on the American government. The interstate opposition was unsuccessful in halting America's invasion of Iraq, but due to the weakness of the USA after the financial crisis and the election of Obama, it may yet prove a method to moderate US foreign policy. Furthermore, some presidential administrations are more amenable to building international consensus than others. George HW Bush and Bill Clinton were far more willing to work through international institutions than George W Bush in the aftermath of September 11. Although pressure from America's international commitments creates a great deal of continuity between administrations, as I have shown there are differences between the foreign policies of Republican and Democratic presidents. Moreover, domestic politics matter. The Tea Party almost led House Republicans to default on America's debt commitment despite pressure from both domestic and international finance. There are of course limitations on how effectively domestic political pressure can challenge elites in the USA, but it is not entirely an unsuccessful method to shape American foreign and domestic policy. Despite the dominance of finance and corporations, the American government is at least somewhat responsive to its citizens if they are organized.

Since the onset of the Great Recession, the USA has been mired in political polarization and conflict. While is not unusual given the culture and institutional design of the USA, the stakes are now extremely high, both for American hegemony and for the capitalist system. The

American government has been central to the promotion and expansion of the free market system, but since 2008, it has been bogged down in politics and infighting. Obama's presidency has led to continual conflict over health care reform, increasing the debt ceiling or passing a budget. If another crisis occurs, with deep divisions between the Republicans and Democrats, its highly likely ideology or partisan interests may win out over the demands of the financial system. America's hegemony may be threatened not due to its lack of responsiveness to crisis rather than any objective economic metric. Leading up to the 2016 presidential election two outsiders, Bernie Sanders and Donald Trump, for the Republican and Democratic nomination respectively have garnered a great deal of attention and support. What they represent is the disillusionment of many Americans with a system that is increasingly unresponsive to their interests.

There is also the distinct possibility neoliberalism may be followed by a more insidious phase of neo-nationalism or, in some countries, neo-fascism. Progressive counter-hegemonic projects have, thus far, been unable to challenge the inequality and economic destabilization from 40 years of neoliberal orthodoxy (Overbeek and van Apeldoorn 2012). Trump and Brexit may not be the aberration but the new norm. Europe and America could go through a phase of reasserting national barriers to trade, bolstering domestic industries, and marginalizing the other and refugees. The USA has a history of slavery, segregation and imprisonment of surplus populations. While it is philosophically committed to liberal values, its history is rife with bigotry, racism and xenophobia. The Trump administration could continue and enhance Obama's policies of mass deportation of illegal, undocumented immigrants. Other presidents, such as Franklin Roosevelt and Ronald Reagan have reshaped the popular discourse in American and global politics: Trump could be a harbinger of a global shift towards a new, more repressive phase in global history.

The paradox of American hegemony is that it has come out of the Great Recession with fewer social, demographic, economic and institutional problems than either China or the European Union, yet it appears to be undergoing an existential crisis. With the election of Donald Trump, along with success of the populist right in other countries, there is yet another impediment to any changes to the political or financial system. Indeed, Breixt and the election of Trump may be a harbinger of the future, as there is a backlash against "elites" and the unequal distribution of economic gains in the post-Great Recession period. It's not inconceivable that America may use its hegemony to pursue a completely different strategy, such as raising tariff barriers, undermining NATO and other major alliances and mass deportations. While it is premature to assume the President will turn campaign rhetoric into policy given the institutional composition of the American political system, the popularity of these ideas and the election of Trump are worrying signs for the stability of American hegemony. His election has sent a signal to other nativist parties throughout the world that their ideas are attractive and they are capable of gaining power. Trump's election will be a test for America's institutions, both those that defend the rights of the marginalized and those that will prevent Trumpism from fracturing the current world order, leaving a power vacuum that could potentially be filled by regional powers. It is not unthinkable for this to take place. As I discussed earlier, one of the reasons for the Great Depression of the 1930s was a lack of American leadership due to the domestic political limitations by US government. This led to an anarchic situation of economic collapse and interstate conflict. History could be repeating itself.

Bibliography

"Interview with Dick Cheney." In *Meet The Press with Tim Russert*, 2003.
"Pentagon News Conference with Donald Rumsfeld." The Pentagon. Washington D.C, 2003.
"Presidential Radio Address, George W. Bush." The Whitehouse. Washington, D.C., 2005.
"Revenue Effects of Major Tax Bills". Edited by United States Department of the Treasury. Washington, DC: Office of Tax Analysis, 2006.
Abedi, A. and Lundberg, T.C. "Doomed to failure? UKIP and the organisational challenges facing right-wing populist anti-political establishment parties." Parliamentary Affairs, 62 (1). 2009: 72–87.
Administration, U.S. Energy Information. "Iraq; Oil Exports." edited by U.S. Energy Information Administration. Washington, DC, 2011.
———. "U.S. Imports by Country of Origin." edited by U.S. Energy Information Administration, 2011.
Agnew, John A. *Hegemony: The New Shape of Global Power*. Philadelphia, [Pa.]: Temple University Press, 2005.
Allegretto, Sylvia A "The State of America's Wealth, 2007" *Economic Policy Institute*, Briefing paper 292, Washington, DC, 2011: 11.
Anderlini, Jamil. "Chinese Property: A Lofty Ceiling." *The Financial Times*, December 13th 2011.
Arrighi, Giovanni. *Adam Smith in Beijing: Lineages of the Twenty-First Century*. London: Verso, 2007.
———. "Hegemony Unraveling-I." *New Left Review* 32 (2005): 23–80.
———. "Hegemony Unraveling-Ii." *New Left Review* 33 (2005): 83–116.
———. *The Long Twentieth Century: Money, Power, and the Origins of Our Times*. [New and updated ed. London: Verso, 2010].

Attané, Isabelle "The Demographic Impact of a Female Deficit in China, 2000–2050." *Population and Development Review* 32, no. 4 (2006): 755–70.
Bacevich, Andrew J. *American Empire: The Realities and Consequences of U.S. Diplomacy.* Cambridge, Mass.: Harvard University Press, 2002.
Bank For International Settlements. "Triennial Central Bank Survey of Foreign Exchange and Derivatives Market Activity 1995 - Final Results", 1996.
Bank For International Settlements. "Amounts Outstanding of over-the-Counter (Otc) Derivatives." In *BIS Quarterly Review*, 2010.
Barandiarán, Edgardo and Leonardo Hernández. "Origins and Resolution of a Banking Crisis in Chile:1982–86." In *Working Papers 57*, edited by Central Bank of Chile. Santiago, Chile, 1999.
Barsky, Robert and Lutz Kilian. "Oil and the Macroeconomy since the 1970s." *National Bureau of Economic Research* Working Paper No. 10855 (October 2004).
Barth, James R, Dan Brumbaugh Jr. and James A. Wilcox "Policy Watch: The Repeal of Glass-Steagall and the Advent of Broad Banking." *The Journal of Economic Perspectives* 14, no. 2 (2000): 191–204.
Beattie, Alan and Tom Braithwaite. "Nations Struggle to Find Consensus on Bank Taxes." *The Financial Times.*, April 24th 2010.
Berg, Peter, Eileen Appelbaum, Thomas Bailey, Arne Kalleberg. "The Performance Effects of Modular Production in the Apparel Industry." *Industrial Relations: A Journal of Economy and Society* 35, no. 3 (1996): 356–73.
Bergoeing, Raphael, Patrick J. Kehoe, Timothy J. Kehoe and Raimundo Soto "Decade Lost and Found: Mexico and Chile in the 1980s." *National Bureau of Economic Research* Working Paper 8520 (2001).
Bernstein, Michael A. *The Great Depression Delayed Recovery and Economic Change in America, 1929–1939.* Cambridge [Cambridgeshire]; New York: Cambridge University Press, 1987.
Bethell, Leslie. *The Cambridge History of Latin America.* New York: Cambridge University Press, 1995.
Bhatia, Michael. "Postconflict Profit: The Political Economy of Intervention." *Global Governance* 11, no. 2 (2005): 205–24.
Blackburn, Simon. *The Oxford Dictionary of Philosophy.* Oxford Paperback Reference. 2nd ed. Oxford; New York: Oxford University Press, 2008.
Boggs, Carl. "Intellectuals and Empire." In *Academic Repression*, edited by Steven Best Anthony Nocella, Peter McLaren. New York: AK Press, 2010.
Bonner, William, and Addison Wiggin. *Empire of Debt: The Rise of an Epic Financial Crisis.* Hoboken, N.J.: Wiley, 2006.
Bordo, Michael, Barry Eichengreen and Jongwoo Kim. "Was There Really an Earlier Period of International Financial Integration Comparable to Today?" *National Bureau of Economic Research* Working Paper 6738 (1998).
Brady, David W, Hahrie Han and Jeremy C. Pope. "Primary Elections and Candidate Ideology: Out of Step with the Primary Electorate?" *Legislative Studies Quarterly*, Vol. 32, No. 1. Feb., 2007. pp. 79–105.

Bamman, David, Brendan O'Connor, Noah Smith. "Censorship and deletion practices in Chinese social media." *First Monday*, [S.l.], March, 2012.
Bremmer, Ian, *Every Nation for Itself: Winners and Losers in a G-Zero World.* New York: Portfolio, 2012.
Buffett, Warren. "2002 Annual Report." edited by Berkshire Hathaway Inc, 2003.
Buhle, Paul. *Marxism in the United States: Remapping the History of the American Left.* Haymarket Series. Rev., 2nd ed. London; New York: Verso, 1991.
Butt, Ronald. "Interview with Margaret Thatcher." *The Sunday Times*, May 1 1981.
Calavita, Kitty and Henry N. Pontell. "Savings and Loan Industry "Heads I Win, Tails You Lose": Deregulation, Crime, and Crisis in the Savings and Loan Industry." *Crime & Delinquency* 36 (1990): 309–41.
Callahan, David. "Think Tanks as Flack." *Washington Monthly*, 1999.
Callinicos, Alex. *Imperialism and Global Political Economy.* Cambridge: Polity, 2009.
Campagna, Anthony S. *The Economic Consequences of the Vietnam War.* New York: Praeger, 1991.
Carlson, Keith and Roger Spencer. "Crowding Out and Its Critics" *Federal Reserve Bank of St. Louis Review*, December 1975, pp. 2–17.
Census1960, U.S. Bureau of the. "Historical Statistics of the United States, Colonial Times to 1957." Washington, D.C.: U.S. Government Printing Office, 1960.
Chernoff, Fred. "Ending the Cold War: The Soviet Retreat and the Us Military Buildup. *International Affairs*, 67, no. 1 (1991): 111–26.
Cho, David and Zachary A. Goldfarb. "U.S. Pushes Ahead with Derivatives Regulation." *The Washington Post*, May 14th 2009.
Chu, Ben. "Thought the worst was over for the economy after Brexit? Think again". *The Independent.* July 5th 2016.
Chomsky, Noam. *American Power and the New Mandarins.* New York: Vintage Books, 1969.
———. *Profit over People: Neoliberalism and Global Order.* 1st ed. New York; Seven Stories Press, 1999.
Christensen, Thomas J. "Fostering Stability or Creating a Monster? The Rise of China and U.S. Policy toward East Asia." *International Security* 31, no. 1 (2006): 81–126.
Clarke, Thomas, and Christos N. Pitelis. *The Political Economy of Privatization.* New York Florence: Routledge Taylor & Francis Group, 1995.
Codevilla, Angelo. "Is Pinochet the Model?". *Foreign Affairs* 72, no. 5 (1993): 127–40.
Cohen, Benjamin J. *The Question of Imperialism: The Political Economy of Dominance and Dependence.* The Political Economy of International Relations Series. New York: Basic Books, 1973.
Cohen, G. A. *Karl Marx's Theory of History: A Defence.* 1st expanded ed. Princeton NJ: Princeton University Press, 2001.

Cohen, Warren I. *America's Response to China: A History of Sino-American Relations*. 5th ed. New York: Columbia University Press, 2010.
Commerce, US Department of. "Us Economy at a Glance: Perspective from the Bea Accounts." edited by US Department of Commerce. Washingston, D.C., 2011.
Confessore, Nicholas. "Total Cost of Election Could Be $6 Billion". *The New York Times*. October 31st, 2012. http://thecaucus.blogs.nytimes.com/2012/10/31/total-cost-of-election-could-be-6-billion/.
Cooper, Helene, Mark Landler and David E. Sanger. " In U.S. Signals to Egypt, Obama Straddled a Rift." *The New York Times*, February 12 2011, A1.
Copeland, Dale C. "Economic Interdependence and War: A Theory of Trade Expectations," *International Security* 20, no. 4 (1996): 208–29.
Corothers, Thomas. "Democracy Promotion under Obama: Finding a Way Forward." Washington, D.C: Carnegie Endowment for International Peace, 2009.
———. "U.S. Democracy Promotion During and after Bush." Washington, D.C.: Carnegie Endowment for International Peace, 2007.
Cortright, David. "A Hard Look at Iraq Sanctions." *The Nation* (November 19 2001).
Curry, Timothy and Lynn Shibut. "The Cost of the Savings and Loan Crisis: Truth and Consequences." In *FDIC Review*, edited by Federal Deposit Insurance Corporation, 26–35. Washington, D.C., 2000.
Christensen, Steen Fryba; Li, Xing. *Emerging Powers, Emerging Markets, Emerging Societies: Global Responses*. ed. / Steen Fryba Christensen; Xing Li. Vol. Part I New York: Palgrave Macmillan, 2016.
Cynamon, Barry Z. and Steven M. Fazzari, "Inequality, the Great Recession, and Slow Recovery" Working Paper: http://ssrn.com/abstract=2205524 or http://dx.doi.org/10.2139/ssrn.2205524.
Daggett, Stephen. "CRS Report to Congress: Costs of Major U.S. Wars" 2008.
DeGrasse Jr, Robert W. and M.E. Sharpe. "Military Expansion Economic Decline: The Impact of Military Spending on U.S. Economic Performance." *Journal of Policy Analysis and Management* 3, no. 3 (1984): 482–83.
Dewen, Wang. "China's Urban and Rural Old Age Security System: Challenges and Options." *China & World Economy* 14, no. 1 (2006): 102–16.
Diamond, Douglas and Philip H. Dybvig. "Bank Runs, Deposit Insurance, and Liquidity." *Journal of Political Economy* 91, no. 3 (June 1983): 401–19.
Dobb, Maurice. "Marxism and the Social Sciences." *Monthly Review* 53, no. 4 (September 2001).
Dolny, Michael. "The Incredible Shrinking Think Tank." *FAIR* March/April 2008 (2008).
Doyle, Michael. "Three Pillars of the Liberal Peace." *American Political Science Review* 99 (2005).
Eaton, Jonathan, Samuel Kortum, Brent Neiman and John Romalis. "Trade and the Global Recession.": The National Bureau of Economic Research, 2011.

Ebell, Monique and James Warren "The Long-Term Economic Impact of Leaving the EU" *National Institute Economic Review May 2016 236: 121–138*.
Economist, The. "The Battle of Smoot-Hawley." December 18th 2008.
———. "China's Tricky Wage Dynamics." *The Economist*, April 5th 2011.
———. "Contagion, What Contagion?" *The Economist*, December 3rd 2011.
———. "The Euro Area's Debt Crisis." *The Economist*, January 12 2011.
———. "Fear of the Dragon." *The Economist.*, January 7th 2010.
———. "Getting to the Naked Truth." *The Economist*, February 12 2012.
———. "The Imf, American and the Euro: Sympathy but No Money." *The Economist*, November 4th 2011.
———. "The Obama Rescue." *The Economist*, February 12th 2009.
———. "The Price of Failure." *The Economist*, October 2nd 2008.
———. "A Short History of Modern Finance." In, (2008).
———. "Take Them Home Responsibly." *The Economist*, Mar 5th 2009.
———. "The Tarp Trap." *The Economist*, November 20th 2008.
———. "The World Economy: Bad, or Worse." *The Economist* October 9th 2008.
Eichengreen, Barry J. *Golden Fetters: The Gold Standard and the Great Depression, 1919-1939*. Nber Series on Long-Term Factors in Economic Development. New York: Oxford University Press, 1992.
Elliot, Larry. "Greece Wouldn't Find It Easy to Leave the Euro." *The Guardian*, April 20th 2010.
Engdahl, F. William. "Greek Guilt and Syriza Perfid" Neo Eastern Outlook. July 16, 2015. http://journal-neo.org/2015/07/16/greek-guilt-and-syriza-perfidy/.
Epstein, Gerald A., Julie Graham, Jessica Gordon Nembhard, and Center for Popular Economics (U.S.). *Creating a New World Economy: Forces of Change and Plans for Action*. Philadelphia: Temple University Press, 1993.
Ernst, Dieter and Linsu Kim. "Global Production Networks, Knowledge Diffusion, and Local Capability Formation." *Research Policy* 31, no. 8–9 (2002): 1417–29.
Esping-Andersen, Gøsta. *The Three Worlds of Welfare Capitalism*. Princeton, N.J.: Princeton University Press, 1990.
Estrin, Saul, Xavier Richet, and Josef C. Brada. *Foreign Direct Investment in Central Eastern Europe: Case Studies of Firms in Transition*. The Microeconomics of Transition Economies. Armonk, N.Y.: M.E. Sharpe, 2000.
Fagan, Richard. "The United States and Chile: Roots and Branches." *Foreign Affairs* 53, no. 2 (1975): 297–313.
Ferguson, Charles H. *Predator Nation: Corporate Criminals, Political Corruption, and the Hijacking of America*. 1st Ed. ed. New York: Crown Business, 2012.
Ferguson, Niall. *The Ascent of Money: A Financial History of the World*. New York: Penguin Books, 2009.
———. *Civilization: The West and the Rest*. 1st American ed. New York: Penguin Press, 2011.

———. *Colossus: The Price of America's Empire.* New York: Penguin Press, 2004.
Ferguson, Thomas. *Legislators Never Bowl Alone: Big Money, Mass Media and the Polarization of Congress.* INET Conference paper. April 2011.
Friedman, John N and Richard T. Holden "The Rising Incumbent Reelection Rate: What's Gerrymandering Got to Do with It?" *The Journal of Politics,* Vol. 71, No. 2 . April., 2009, pp. 593-611.
Fisher, Jonas D.M and Andreas Hornstein "The Role of Real Wages, Productivity, and Fiscal Policy in Germany's Great Depression 1928–1937." *Review of Economic Dynamics* 5, no. 1 (2002): 100–27.
Foster, John Bellamy, and Fred Magdoff. *The Great Financial Crisis: Causes and Consequences.* New York: Monthly Review Press, 2009.
France-Presse, Agence. "Iraq Oil Exports Highest since Saddam: Ministry". *AFP* February, 23 2011.
Friedberg, Aaron L. "The Future of U.S.-China Relations: Is Confict Inevitable?". *International Security* 30, no. 2 (2005): 7–45.
Friedman, Benjamin M. "Deficits and Debt in the Short and Long Run." edited by National Bureau of Economic Research., 1–37, 2005.
Friedman, Milton, Anna Jacobson Schwartz, and National Bureau of Economic Research. *The Great Contraction, 1929–1933.* Princeton Paperbacks. 1st Princeton paperback ed. Princeton, N.J.: Princeton University Press, 1965.
Friedman Thomas and Michael Mandelbaum. *That Used to Be Us.* New York: Farrar, Straus and Giroux, 2011.
Froud, Julie. *Financialization and Strategy: Narrative and Numbers.* London; New York: Routledge, 2006.
Frum, David, and Richard Norman Perle. *An End to Evil: How to Win the War on Terror.* 1st mass market ed. New York: Ballantine, 2004.
Fukuyama, Francis. *The End of History and the Last Man.* New York: HarperCollins, 2002.
Fund, International Monetary. "World Economic Outlook Database - October 2010: Nominal Gdp List of Countries," edited by International Monetary Fund, 2010.
Gaddis, John Lewis. *The Cold War: A New History.* New York: Penguin Press, 2005.
———. *Strategies of Containment: A Critical Appraisal of American National Security Policy During the Cold War.* Rev. and expanded ed. New York: Oxford University Press, 2005.
Gan, Nectar. "Chinese protest against incinerator plant turns violent" South China Morning Post. July 3rd, 2016. http://www.scmp.com/news/china/policies-politics/article/1984955/chinese-protest-against-incinerator-plant-turns-violent.
Gapper, John. "Tarp Travels Down a Hazardous Road." *The Financial Times,* December 8th 2009.

Gertz, Bill. "Chinese See U.S. Debt as Weapon in Taiwan Dispute," *The Washington Post*, February 10th 2010.

Giddens, Anthony. *The Third Way: The Renewal of Social Democracy*. Cambridge, UK; Malden, Mass.: Polity Press, 1998.

Gill, Stephen. "Economic Globalization and the Internationalization of Authority: Limits and Contradictions." *Geoforum* 23, no. 3 (1992): 269–84.

Giroux, Henry A. *The University in Chains: Confronting the Military-Industrial-Academic Complex*. The Radical Imagination Series. Boulder, CO: Paradigm Publishers, 2007.

Glenn, John. *China's Challenge to US Supremacy*. New York: Palgrave MacMillan, 2017.

Goldberg, Peter A. "The Politics of the Allende Overthrow in Chile." *Political Science Quarterly*, 90, no. 1 (1975): 3–116.

Goodwin, Matthew; Milazzo, Caitlin. *UKIP: Inside the Campaign to Redraw the Map of British Politics*. Oxford: Oxford University Press. 2015.

Goodwin, Matthew. "Ukip, the 2015 General Election and Britain's EU Referendum". *Parliamentary Insight*. 6 (3). 2015: 12–15.

Gordon, Adam. "The Creation of Homeownership: How New Deal Changes in Banking Regulation Simultaneously Made Homeownership Accessible to Whites and out of Reach for Blacks." *The Yale Law Journal* 115, no. 1 (2005): 186–226.

Gourevitch, Peter Alexis. *Politics in Hard Times: Comparative Responses to International Economic Crises*. Cornell Studies in Political Economy. Ithaca: Cornell University Press, 1986.

Gowan, Peter. "Economics and Politics within the Capitalist Core and the Debate on the New Imperialism." (2005).

Goyala, Vidhan K, Kenneth Lehnb and Stanko Racicb. "Growth Opportunities and Corporate Debt Policy: The Case of the U.S. Defense Industry." *Journal of Financial Economics* 64, no. 1 (2002): 35–59.

Graham, David. "How Big Money Created the Most Polarized Congress in a Century" The Atlantic. July 9th 2013. http://www.theatlantic.com/politics/archive/2013/07/how-big-money-created-the-most-polarized-congress-in-a-century-5-charts/277611/.

Greven, Thomas. *The Rise of Right-wing Populism in Europe and the United States*. Friedrich-Ebert-Stiftung. Washington, DC. May 2016.

Hager, Sandy Brian "America's Real 'Debt Dilemma'", *Review of Capital as Power*, Vol. 1, No. 1, 2013, pp. 42–65.

Hardt, Michael, and Antonio Negri. *Multitude: War and Democracy in the Age of Empire*. New York: Penguin Press, 2004.

Hardt, Michael, and Antonio Negri. *Empire*. Cambridge, Mass.: Harvard University Press, 2000.

Harvey, David. *A Brief History of Neoliberalism*. New York: Oxford University Press, 2007.
———. *A Brief History of Neoliberalism*. Oxford: Oxford University Press, 2005.
———. *The Enigma of Capital: And the Crises of Capitalism*. Pbk. ed. Oxford; New York: Oxford University Press, 2011.
———. *The Limits to Capital*. London: Verso, 2006.
———. *The New Imperialism*. Oxford; New York: Oxford University Press, 2005.
Hayton, Richard. "Towards the Mainstream? UKIP and the 2009 Elections to the European Parliament." *Politics, 30. 2010*: 26–35.
Hazell, Robert and Alen Renwick. "Brexit: Its Consequences for Devolution and the Union" UCL Constitution Briefing paper. May 19, 2016.
Helleiner, Eric. "Explaining the Globalization of Financial Markets: Bringing States Back In." *Review of International Political Economy* 2, no. 2 (1995): 315–42.
———. *States and the Reemergence of Global Finance: From Bretton Woods to the 1990s*. Ithaca, NY: Cornell University Press, 1994.
_____ *The Status Quo Crisis: Global Financial Governance After the 2008 Meltdown*. New York: Oxford University Press, 2014.
Helleiner, Eric and Stefano Pagliari "The End of Self Regulation?". In *Global Finance in Crisis*, edited by Stefano Pagliari Eric Helleiner, Hubert Zimmerman. New York: Routledge, 2010.
Henning, C. Randall. *Currencies and Politics in the United States, Germany, and Japan*. Washington, DC: Institute for International Economics, 1994.
Hernandez, Javier, "Labor Protests Multiply in China as Economy Slows, Worrying Leaders" The New York Times. March 14, 2016, A01.
Hesketh, Therese and Zhu Wei Xing. "Abnormal Sex Ratios in Human Populations: Causes and Consequence." *Proceedings of the National Academy of Science*, 103, no. 36 (2006): 13271–75.
Horby, Lucy. "China coal protests highlight overcapacity tensions." The Financial Times. March 13th, 2016. https://www.ft.com/content/1f8519fe-e8cd-11e5-bb79-2303682345c8.
Howard, M.C. and J.E. King *The Rise of Neoliberalism in Advanced Capitalism Economies*. New York: Palgrave-Macmillan, 2008.
Hulse, Carl and Adam Nagourney. "Obama's Afghanistan Decision Is Straining Ties with Democrats." *The New York Times*. December 3 2009, A20.
Ignatieff, Michael. *Empire Lite: Nation-Building in Bosnia, Kosovo and Afghanistan*. Toronto: Penguin Canada, 2003.
Ikenberry, G John. "Institutions, Strategic Restraint, and the Persistence of American Postwar Order." *International Security* 23, no. 3 (1998): 43–78.
Ikenberry, G John and Anne Marie Slaughter. "Forging a World of Liberty under Law. Us National Security in the 21st Centur." edited by Princeton Project on National Security. New Jersey, 2006.

Jensen Mads Dagnis and Holly Snaith "When politics prevails: the political economy of a Brexit" Journal of European Public Policy Volume 23, 9, 2016: 1302–1310.
Johnson, Leland. "U.S. Business Interests in Cuba and the Rise of Castro." *World Politics.* 17, no. 3 (1965): 440–59.
Journal, The Wall Street. "Dow Jones Industrial Average All-Time Largest One Day Gains and Losses." In, *Historical Data Index* (2011). http://online.wsj.com/mdc/public/page/2_3047-djia_alltime.html.
Kaltefleiter, Caroline and Mechthild Nagel. "The Carceral Society." In *Academic Repression*, edited by Steven Best Anthony Nocella, Peter McLaren. New York: AK Press, 2010.
Katznelson, Ira, Kim Geiger and Daniel Kryder. "Limiting Liberalism: The Southern Veto in Congress, 1933–1950." *Political Science Quarterly* 108, no. 2 (1993): 283–306.
Kaufman, Robert Gordon. *In Defense of the Bush Doctrine.* Lexington, Ky.: University Press of Kentucky, 2007.
Keister, Lisa and Stephanie Moller "Wealth Inequality in the United States." *Annual Review of Sociology* 26 (2000): 63–81.
Keohane, Robert O., and Joseph S. Nye. *Power and Interdependence.* 3rd ed. New York: Longman, 2001.
Keynes, John Maynard. *The General Theory of Employment, Interest and Money.* London: Macmillan, 1936.
Kindleberger, Charles Poor. *The World in Depression, 1929-1939.* History of the World Economy in the Twentieth Century, V. 4. Berkeley,: University of California Press, 1973.
King, Gary, Robert O. Keohane, and Sidney Verba. *Designing Social Inquiry: Scientific Inference in Qualitative Research.* Princeton, N.J.: Princeton University Press, 1994.
Klein, Naomi. *No Logo: No Space, No Choice, No Jobs: Taking Aim at the Brand Bullies.* London: Flamingo, 2000.
Kowalcky, Linda W.; LeLoup, Lance T. "Congress and the Politics of Statutory Debt Limitation". *Public Administration Review* Vol. 53 No. 1. 1993.
Krauthammer, Charles. "Our Salutary Debt-Ceiling Scare." *National Review*, June 3 2011.
Krugman, Paul. "The Obama Gap." *The New York Times*, January 8th 2009.
———. "Wall Street Whitewash." *The New York Times*, December 17 2010, A39.
Kwon, O. Yul "Korean Economic Developments and Prospects." *Pacific Economic Literature* 11, no. 12 (1997): 15–39.
Labour, United States Department of. "Employment Situation Summary." edited by United States Department of Labour. Washington, D.C., 2010.
Lambrecht, Bart M. "The Impact of Debt Financing on Entry and Exit in a Duopoly." *Review of Financial Studies* 14, no. 3 (2001): 765–804.

Lapid, Yosef. "The Third Debate: On the Prospects of International Theory in a Post-Positivist Era." *International Studies Quarterly* 33 (1989): 235-54.

Layne, Christopher. "Offshore Balancing Revisited." *The Washington Quarterly* 25, no. 1 (2002): 233–48.

———. "The Unipolar Illusion Revisited: The Coming End of the United States' Unipolar Moment." *International Security* 31, no. 3 (2006): 7–41.

Layne, Christopher, and Bradley A. Thayer. *American Empire: A Debate*. New York: Routledge, 2007.

Layman, Geoffrey C, and Thomas M. Carsey "Party Polarization and 'Conflict Extension' in the American Electorate" *American Journal of Political Science*, Vol. 46, No. 4. October., 2002, pp. 786–802.

Levit, Mindy R., Clinton T. Brass, Thomas J. Nicola, Dawn Nuschler, Alison M. Shelton. "Reaching the Debt Limit: Background and Potential Effects on Government Operations". *Congressional Research Service*. Washington, D.C. May 31st 2012.

Lieberson, Stanley. "An Empirical Study of Military-Industrial Linkages". *American Journal of Sociology* 76, no. 4 (1971): 562–84.

Lilley, Brian. "Ignatieff Linked to Iraq War Planning." *Edmonton Sun*, Wednesday, April 20th 2011.

Lucas, Robert E. Jr. and Leonard A. Rapping "Unemployment in the Great Depression: Is There a Full Explanation?". *Journal of Political Economy* 80, no. 1 (January-Feburary 1972): 186–91.

Luxberg, Steve. "Bob Woodward Book Details Obama Battles with Advisers over Exit Plan for Afghan War". *The Washingston Post*, September 22 2010.

Mabee, Bryan "Discourses of Empire: The Us 'Empire'." *Third World Quarterly* 25, no. 8 (2004): 1359–78.

MacMillan, Margaret. *Paris 1919: Six Months That Changed the World*. Random House Trade paperback ed. New York: Random House, 2003.

Maitland, Maureen and David Blitzer. "S&P/Case-Shiller Home Price Indices 2010, a Year in Review." In, *S&P Indices; a Year in Review* (2011). Published electronically January. http://www.standardandpoors.com.

Maliszewski, Wojciech, Serkan Arslanalp, John Caparusso, José Garrido, Si Guo, Joong Shik Kang, W. Raphael Lam, T. Daniel Law, Wei Liao, Nadia Rendak, Philippe Wingender, Jiangyan Yu, and Longmei Zhang. "Resolving China's Corporate Debt Problem". IMF Working Paper. The International Monetary Fund. 2016.

Mamudi, Sam. "Lehman Folds with Record $613 Billion Debt." *Marketwatch*, September 15 2008.

Mandelbaum, Michael. *The Case for Goliath: How America Acts as the World's Government in the Twenty-First Century*. 1st ed. New York: PublicAffairs, 2005.

Markwell, Donald. *John Maynard Keynes and International Relations: Economic Paths to War and Peace*. Oxford; New York: Oxford University Press, 2006.

Marx, Karl. *Capital: A Critique of Political Economy.* Moscow: Progress Publishers, 1984.
———. *Capital Volume 3.* New York: International Publishers, 1996. http://www.marxists.org/archive/marx/works/1894-c3/ch29.htm.
———. *Economic and Philosophic Manuscripts of 1844.* New York: International Publishers, 1969.
———. "The Eighteenth Brumaire of Louis Bonaparte. Karl Marx 1852." In *Karl Marx: A Reader*, edited by Jon Elster. Cambridge: Cambridge University Press, 1986.
———. *Grundrisse: Foundations of the Critique of Political Economy.* New York: Penguin, 1993.
———. *Value: Studies.* London New York: New Park Publications; distributed by Labor Publications, 1976.
Marx, Karl and Jon Elster. *Karl Marx: A Reader.* Cambridge: Cambridge University Press, 1986.
Mayerson, Harold. "Bush the Incompetent." *The Washington Post*, January 25 2006.
Mearsheimer, John. "Hans Morgenthau and the Iraq War: Realism Versus Neo-Conservatism." Opendemocracy.com, http://www.opendemocracy.net/democracy-americanpower/morgenthau_2522.jsp.
Mearsheimer, John J., and Stephen Walt. "An Unnecessary War." *Foreign Policy* 134, no. January-Februrary (2003): 51-59.
Mehrling, Perry. *Fischer Black and the Revolutionary Idea of Finance.* Hoboken, N.J.: John Wiley & Sons, 2005.
Minter, Adam. "Where are the Protests in China?" Bloomberg LP. July 13th, 2016. https://www.bloomberg.com/view/articles/2016-07-13/why-china-doesn-t-want-south-china-sea-protests.
Mitra, Pradeep, Marcelo Selowsky, and Juan Zalduendo. *Turmoil at Twenty: Recession, Recovery, and Reform in Central and Eastern Europe and the Former Soviet Union.* Washington, DC: World Bank, 2010.
Montgomery, Lori, and Rosalind S. Helderman. "Obama signs bill to raise debt limit, reopen government." *The Washington Post.* October 16th, 2013.
Moore, David. "Hardt and Negri's Empire and Real Empire: The Terrors of 9-11 and After." *ACME: An International E-Journal for Critical Geographies* 2, no. 2 (2003): 112–31.
Moy, Joyanna. "Recent Trends in Unemployment and the Labor Force: 10 Countries." *Monthly Labor Review Bureau of Labor Statistics* 108, no. 8 (1985): 9–22.
Münkler, Herfried. *Empires: The Logic of World Domination from Ancient Rome to the United States* [in Translated from the German.]. Cambridge: Polity, 2007.
Murphy, Craig. "The Promise of Critical Ir, Partially Kept." *Review of International Studies* 33 (2007): 117–33.
Murray, Williamson, and Allan Reed Millett. *Military Innovation in the Interwar Period.* Cambridge; New York: Cambridge University Press, 1996.

Nash, Robert. T and William P Gramm "A Neglected Early Statement the Paradox of Thrift". *History of Political Economy* Vol. 1 No. 2, 1969: 395–400.
News, BBC Business. "Euro Falls on Rumours Greece Is to Quit the Eurozone." *BBC News Magazine*, May 7th 2011.
New York Times "How the Tea Party Fared". *The New York Times.* November 4th, 2010.
Nordlund, Willis J. *Silent Skies: The Air Traffic Controllers' Strike.* Westport, Conn: Praeger, 1998.
O'Meara, Dan ed. *Hegemony, Militarism and Identity.* edited by Bruno Charbonneau and Wayne S. Cox, Locating Global Order. Vancouver: UBC Press, 2010.
O'Reilly, Kenneth "Mccarthy Era Blacklisting of School Teachers, College Professors, and Other Public Employees." edited by Federal Bureau of Investigation, 24. Washington, D.C.: University Publications of America, 1989.
Oesch, Daniel. "Explaining Workers' Support *for* Right-Wing Populist Parties *in* Western Europe: Evidence *from* Austria, Belgium, France, Norway, *and* Switzerland." *International Political Science Review.* vol. 29, no. 3. 2008: 349–373.
Organization, The International Labour. "Global Employment Trends, January 2010." Geneva: The International Labour Organization, 2010.
Overbeek, Henk, and Bastiaan van Apeldoorn. *Neoliberalism in Crisis.* New York: Palgrave Macmillan, 2012.
Overholt, William. "China in the Global Financial Crisis: Rising Influence, Rising Challenges." *Washington Quarterly.* 33, no. 1 (2010): 21–34.
P.W., Singer. "Factories to Call Our Own." *The Washingtonian*, 2010.
Paletta, Damian. "Where they Stand on Foreign Policy Issues". *The Wall Street Journal.* 2016. http://graphics.wsj.com/elections/2016/donald-trump-hillary-clinton-on-foreign-policy/.
Panitch, Leo, and Sam Gindin. *Global Capitalism and American Empire.* London [Black Point, N.S.]: Merlin Press; Fernwood Pub., 2004.
Panitch, Leo, and Sam Gindin, *The Making of Global Capitalism.* New York: Verso, 2012.
Panitch, Leo, and Martijn Konings. *American Empire and the Political Economy of Global Finance.* International Political Economy Series. Basingstoke; New York: Palgrave Macmillan, 2009.
Parker, George and Tony Barber. "European Call for 'Bretton Woods Ii'." *The Financial Times*, October 16 2008.
Parsons, Craig. *A Certain Idea of Europe.* Cornell Studies in Political Economy. Ithaca: Cornell University Press, 2003.
Pastor, Jr, Manuel. "Latin America, the Debt Crisis, and the International Monetary Fund." *Latin American Perspectives* 16, no. 1 (1989): 79–110.
Paterson, Thomas G. "The Origins of the Cold War." *OAH Magazine of History* 2, no. 1 (1986): 5–9.

Peel, Quentin. "Eurozone Set for Fiscal Union, Says Merkel." *Financial Times*, December 14th 2011.
Pierson, Paul. "When Effect Becomes Cause: Policy Feedback and Political Chang E the Three Worlds of Welfare Capitalism by Gosta Esping-Andersen; the Political Power of Economic Ideas: Keynesianism across Countries by Peter Hall; Institutions, Institutional Change and Economic Performance by Douglass C. North; Protecting Soldiers and Mothers: The Political Origins of Social Policy in the United States by Theda Skocpol." *World Politics* 45, no. 4 (1993): 595–628.
Pingali, Prabhu L. and Vo-Tong Xuan. "Vietnam: Decollectivization and Rice Productivity Growth." *Economic Development and Cultural Change* 40, no. 4 (1992): 697–718.
Polanyi, Karl. *The Great Transformation: The Political and Economic Origins of Our Time*. 2nd Beacon Paperback ed. Boston, Mass.: Beacon Press, 2001.
Politi, James. "Us Retreats from Brink of Debt Default." *The Financial Times*, August 3rd 2011.
Posner, Elliot "European Approach to Financial Regulation." In *Global Finance in Crisis*, edited by Stefano Pagliari Eric Helleiner, Hubert Zimmerman. 108–20. New York: Routeledge, 2010.
Prasad, Enwar, *The Dollar Trap*. Princeton: Princeton University Press, 2014.
Rhoades, Gary and Sheila Slaughter. "Academic Capitalism, Managed Professionals, and Supply-Side Higher Education." *Social Texts* 51 (1997): 9–38.
Ricci, David M. *The Tragedy of Political Science: Politics, Scholarship, and Democracy*. New Haven, CT: Yale University Press, 1984.
Roberts, Dexter. "China's Growing Income Gap." *Bloomberg Businessweek*, January 27th 2011.
Roberts, Russell. "How Government Stoked the Mania." *The Wall Street Journal*, October 3rd 2008.
Robinson, William I. *Promoting Polyarchy: Globalization, Us Intervention, and Hegemony*. Cambridge Studies in International Relations. Cambridge [England]; New York: Cambridge University Press, 1996.
———. *A Theory of Global Capitalism: Production, Class, and State in a Transnational World*. Themes in Global Social Change. Baltimore: Johns Hopkins University Press, 2004.
Romer, Christina, and David Romer. *Reducing Inflation: Motivation and Strategy*. Studies in Business Cycles. Chicago: University of Chicago Press, 1997.
Rooduijn, M. "The rise of the populist radical right in Western Europe" *European View*. 14: 3. 2015.
Rupert, Mark. "Academia and the Culture of Repression." In *Academic Repression* edited by Steven Best Anthony Nocella, Peter McLaren. New York: AK Press, 2010.

Russel, Bruce. "Bushwacking the Democratic Peace." *International Studies Perspectives* 6, no. 4 (November 2005): 395–408.

Russel, Richard. "American Diplomatic Realism: A Tradition Practised and Preached." *Diplomacy & Statecraft* 11, no. 3 (November 2000): 159–82.

Sachs, J, A Tornell and Andrés Velasco. "The Mexican Peso Crisis: Sudden Death or Death Foretold?". *Journal of International Economics.* 41, no. 3–4 (1996): 265-83.

Said, Edward W. *Orientalism.* 25th anniversary ed. New York: Vintage Books, 2003.

Sargent, James E. "The Plot to Seize the White House." *The History Teacher* 8, no. 1 (1974): 151–52.

Sassen, Saskia. "Global Financial Centers." *Foreign Affairs* 78, no. 1 (1999): 75–87.

Sayer, Derek. *Marx's Method: Ideology, Science and Critique in Capital.* 2nd ed. Brighton, N.J.: Harvester; Humanities Press, 1983.

———. *The Violence of Abstraction: The Analytic Foundations of Historical Materialism.* Oxford: B. Blackwell, 1987.

Schlesinger, Arthur Meier. *The Coming of the New Deal, 1933–1935.* Boston Houghton Mifflin, 1957.

Schmidt, Brian C. *The Political Discourse of Anarchy a Disciplinary History of International Relations.* Albany: State University of New York Press, 1998.

Schwartz, Herman. "Housing, Global Finance, and American Hegemony: Building Conservative Politics One Brick at a Time." *Comparative European Politics* 6 (2008): 262–84.

Schwartz, Nelson. "Wages Rise as U.S. Unemployment Rate Falls Below 5%". *The New York Times.* February 5, 2016, B6.

Seacor, Jesica. "Environmental Terrorism: Lessons from the Oil Fire of Kuwait". *American University Journal of International Law and Policy.* 10, no. 1 (1994): 481-523.

Shambaugh, David L. *China Goes Global.* New York: Oxford University Press, 2013.

———. "The Coming Chinese Crack Up" *The Wall Street Journal.* March 16th, 2015.

Shih, Victor C. *Factions and Finance in China: Elite Conflict and Inflation.* Cambridge; New York: Cambridge University Press, 2008.

Singer, PW. "Factories to Call Our Own." *The Washingtonian*, 2010.

———. "Outsourcing War." *Foreign Affairs* 84 (2005).

Silver, Nate. "Dear Media, Stop Freaking Out About Donald Trump's Polls". Five Thirty Eight. November 23rd, 2015. http://fivethirtyeight.com/features/dear-media-stop-freaking-out-about-donald-trumps-polls/.

Skocpol, Theda "Political Response to Capitalist Crisis." *Politics & Society* 10, no. 2 (1980): 155–201.

Smith, Tony. "Decolonization and the Response of Colonial Elites. "*Comparative Studies in Society and History* 20, no. 1 (1978): 70–102.

Sorkin, Andrew Ross. "Lehman Files for Bankruptcy; Merrill Is Sold." *The New York Times*, September 14th 2008, A1.

———. *Too Big to Fail: The inside Story of How Wall Street and Washington Fought to Save the Financial System--and Themselves*. New York: Viking, 2009.

Stephanson, Anders. *Manifest Destiny: American Expansionism and the Empire of Right*. 1st ed. New York: Hill and Wang, 1995.

Steinhouer, Jennifer. "Congress Nearing End of Session Where Partisan Input Impeded Output" *The New York Times*. September 18, 2012.

Steinhauser, Paul and Robert Yoon, "Cost to win congressional election skyrockets" CNN politics. July 11, 2013.

Steinhauser, Paul. "CNN Poll: Majority says raise debt ceiling" CNN politics. October 2, 2013.

Sterns, Peter *Consumer Society in World History*. New York: Routledge, 2001.

Stavrakakis, Yannis and Giorgos Katsambekis "Left-wing populism in the European periphery: the case of SYRIZA" Journal of Political Ideologies, 19:2, 2014: 119–142.

Stiglitz, Joseph and Linda J. Bilmes. "The True Cost of the Iraq War: $3 Trillion and Beyond." *Washingston Post*, September 5 2010.

Stiglitz, Joseph E. *Globalization and Its Discontents*. New York: W.W. Norton, 2003.

Stokesbury, James L. *A Short History of World War I*. 1st ed. New York: Morrow, 1980.

Stolberg, Sheryl Gay and Helene Cooper. "Obama Adds Troops but Maps Exit." *The New York Times*, December 1 2009, A1.

Stubbs, Richard. "War and Economic Development: Export-Oriented Industrialization in East and Southeast Asia." *Comparative Politics* 31, no. 3 (1999): 337–55.

Stueck, William Whitney. *The Korean War: An International History*. Princeton Studies in International History and Politics. Princeton, N.J.: Princeton University Press, 1995.

Surowiecki, James. "How will Brexit Shake Out?" The New Yorker. July 17, 2016. http://www.newyorker.com/magazine/2016/07/11/the-economics-of-brexit.

Taylor, Brendan. "The Bush Administration and Asia Pacific Multilateralism: Unrequited Love?". *Australian Journal of International Affairs* 62, no. 1 (2006): 1–15.

Teicher, Howard, and Gayle Radley Teicher. *Twin Pillars to Desert Storm: America's Flawed Vision in the Middle East from Nixon to Bush*. New York: William Morrow and Co., 1993.

Telegraph, The. "Chinese Gender Imbalance Will Leave Millions of Men without Wives." *The Telegraph*, 2011.

Tesler, Michael. "Trump is the first modern Republican to win the nomination based on racial prejudice" The Washington Post. August 1st 2016. https://www.washingtonpost.com/news/monkey-cage/wp/2016/08/01/trump-is-the-first-republican-in-modern-times-to-win-the-partys-nomination-on-anti-minority-sentiments/.

Thayer, Bradley A. "In Defense of Primacy." *The National Interest* (November-December 2006).

Tilley, Ian. "Bernanke Warns on Debt-Limit 'Chaos'." *The Wall Street Journal*, March 1st 2011.

Traub, James. "The World According to Barack Obama." *Foreign Policy Magazine*, June 1 2010.

Travieso-Diaz, Matias and Charles F. Trumbull IV. "Foreign Investment in Cuba: Prospects and Perils". *George Washington International Law Review* 35, no. 4 (2003): 903-36.

Turner, Graham, and GFC Economics. *The Credit Crunch: Housing Bubbles, Globalisation and the Worldwide Economic Crisis.* London: Pluto Press, in association with GFC Economics, 2008.

United States Department of the Treasury. "Major Foreign Holders of US Treasuries" 2014. http://www.treasury.gov/resource-center/data-chart-center/tic/Documents/mfh.txt.

United States Federal Reserve Board. *Changes in U.S. Family Finances from 2007 to 2010: Evidence from the Survey of Consumer Finance.* 2012: 2.

Vermerien, Mattias, *Power and Imbalances in the Global Monetary System.* London: Palgrave MacMillan, 2014. A Comparative Capitalism Perspective.

Waever, Ole. "The Sociology of a Not So International Discipline: American and European Developments in International Relations." *International Organization* 52, no. 4 (2005): 687–727.

Waggoner, John "Subprime Woes Could Spill over into Other Sectors." *USA Today*, March 15 2007.

Walker, RBJ. "History and Structure in the Theory of International Relations." *Millennium – Journal of International Studies* 18, no. 2 (1989): 163–83.

Wallace, Michael. "Aggressive Economism, Defensive Control: Contours of American Labour Militancy, 1947–81." *Economic and Industrial Democracy* 10, no. 1 (1989): 7–34.

Walt, Vivienne. "U.S. Companies Shut out as Iraq Auctions Its Oil Fields." *Time Magazine*, December 10 2009.

Waltz, Kenneth Neal. *Theory of International Politics.* 1st ed. New York: Random House, 1979.

Weaver, Joyce. "Point. Click. Matriculate." *Libri* 49 (1999): 142–49.

Weiler, Michael and W. Barnett Pearce. *Reagan and Public Discourse in America* Tuscaloosa: University of Alabama Press, 1992.

White, Lawrence J. "A Cautionary Tale of Deregulation Gone Awry: The S&L Debacle". *Southern Economic Journal* 59, no. 3 (1993): 496–514.

Whyte, Martin, "Paradoxes of China's Economic Boom". *The Annual Review of Sociology.* 2009. 35: 371–92.

Williams, Timothy. "Sunnis in Iraq Allied with U.S. Rejoin Rebels." *The New York Times*, October 16 2010, A1.

Williamson, John. "What Should the World Bank Think About the Washington Consensus?", edited by Peterson Institute for International Economics: World Bank's World Development Report 2000, 1999.

Winterton, Jonathan, and Ruth Winterton. *Coal, Crisis, and Conflict: The 1984-85 Miners' Strike Inyorkshire*. Manchester; New York New York: Manchester University Press; St. Martin's Press, 1989.

Wiseman, Jonathan, and Ashley Parker. "House Approves Higher Debt Limit Without Condition." *The New York Times*. Feb11, 2014.

Wohlforth, William. "The Stability of a Unipolar World." *International Security* 24, no. 2 (Summer 1999): 5-41.

Wood, Ellen Meiksins. *Empire of Capital*. London; New York: VERSO, 2003.

———. *The Origin of Capitalism: A Longer View*. London New York: Verso, 2002.

Worldfactbook, CIA. "Country Comparison: Gdp - Per Capita (Ppp)." Washington, D.C: Central Intelligence Agency, 2010.

Young, Angelo. "Cost of Sequestering" *International Business Times*. February 20th, 2013.

Zahrani, Mostafa T. "The Coup That Changed the Middle East: Mossadeq V. The Cia in Retrospect." *World Policy Journal*. 19, no. 2 (2002): 93-99.

Zakaria, Fareed. *The Post-American world*. New York: W.W. Norton & Co., 2009.

Index

A
Air traffic controllers strike, 1981, 60
Arrighi, Giovanni, 39, 91

B
Bremmer, Ian, 4
Bretton Woods, 5, 13, 22, 37, 40, 47, 59, 102, 114, 117, 123, 127
  End of, 47
Brexit, 3, 74–77, 120, 133

C
Canada
  impact of financial crisis, 132
Chilean coup 1973, 35
China
  demographics, 8
  financial instability, 8
  home prices, 106
  one child policy, 82
  opening, 65
  People's Bank, 80
  protests, 87, 88
  rise in inequality, 82
  stock market crisis, 100
  US interdependence, 88
  US tensions, 94
  US treasury holdings, 99
Christensen and Xing, 3, 79, 89
Citizens United Versus FEC (2011), 150, 153
Cold war
  end of, 49
Congressional stagnation, 111
Credit Default Swaps, 96
Cuban revolution, 27

D
Debt ceiling
  2011 crisis, 107
  2013, 109
  consequences, 120
  impact on China, 117

E
Eichengreen, Barry, 37, 38, 40

Euro
  limits on monetary policy, 85
  origins, 116
European Central Bank, 6, 68

F
Ferguson, Niall, 4, 39, 80, 91
French National Front, 7
Friedman, Milton, 34
Friedman, Thomas, 4

G
General Agreement on Tariffs
  and Trade. *See* World Trade
  Organization
Gindin, Sam, 4, 40, 68, 95, 102, 103, 123
Glass-Steagall Act of 1933, 18
The gold standard, 15, 21, 34
Gorbachev, Mikhail, 88
The Great Depression, 2, 4, 13, 14, 18–21, 30, 37, 38, 97, 106, 127, 129, 134
  banking failures, 16
  protectionism, 24
The Great Recession
  centrality of the US dollar, 115
  mortgage crisis, 106
  US government's role, 132
Greece
  financial crisis, 6, 9, 10, 90, 92–94, 100, 102, 103

H
Harvey, David, 122
Hayek, FV, 30, 34
Helleiner, Eric, 2, 4, 40, 61, 78, 106, 114–116, 121, 123

Hungary
  right wing nationalism, 7

I
International Monetary Fund
  debt crisis of the 1980s, 48

K
Keynes, John Maynard, 22, 38
Kindleberger, Charles, 11, 38
Korean war, 5, 25, 26, 39
  after effects, 37

L
Lehman Brothers, 5, 85, 94, 96, 99–101, 103, 104, 121

M
Macmillan, Margaret, 37
Mandelbaum, Michael, 4
Marx, Karl, 122
  Marxist theory, 24
Mexican peso crisis, 62
Moral hazard, 103

N
Neoliberalism
  acceptance by the left, 56
  American state's role, 68
  Chile, 48
  Friedman, Milton, 37
  origins, 5
  The Reagan administration, 34
  spread to Eastern Europe, 120
  technology, 49
Nixon, Richard

economic policy, 59

O
Obama administration
  quantitative easing, 116
Oil embargo, 33

P
Panitch, Leo, 4, 40, 68, 95, 102, 103, 123
PIIGS, 6, 66, 69, 71, 131
Planned economies
  after the Second World War, 32
Poland
  right wing nationalism, 10

R
Reagan, Ronald, 13, 44, 49, 50, 60, 133
Roosevelt, Franklin, 17–21, 107, 133
  The New Deal, 20

S
Savings and Loan Bailout, 46, 60
Second World War, 1, 2, 4, 20, 21, 24, 25, 29, 32, 50, 58, 120, 127, 129
Shambaugh, David, 3, 80, 88
Sino-Soviet Split, 51
Stagflation, 33
Subprime mortages, 106

T
TARP, 123, 124
The Tea Party, 2, 10, 112, 117, 120, 122, 129, 132

Thatcher, Margaret, 14, 46, 47, 60
The Third Way
  Blair, Tony, 52
Trump, Donald, 2
  economic promises, 119
  potential global disruption, 98
  Republican primary, 119
  rise in popularity, 134

U
UK Coal Miners Strike, 1984–1985, 46
United Kingdom Independence Party, 7, 72–75
US debt
  China's role, 121

V
Vermeiren, Mattias, 4
Vietnam war, 5
  economic costs, 46
  US economic interests, 24
Volcker, Paul, 44

W
War on Terror, 5
  Al Qaeda, 14, 56
  economic effects, 131
  Iraq war, 58
  oil interests, 89
  September 11th, 2001, 55
World Trade Organization, 54
  origins, 5

Z
Zakaria, Fareed, 4

CPSIA information can be obtained
at www.ICGtesting.com
Printed in the USA
LVOW13*1825201017
553176LV00013B/292/P

9 781137 575388